# SCOTTISH MONASTERIES

# SCOTTISH MONASTERIES

*in the Late Middle Ages*

MARK DILWORTH

EDINBURGH UNIVERSITY PRESS

Edinburgh University Press Ltd
22 George Square, Edinburgh

Typeset in Linotron Caledonia
by Nene Phototypesetters Ltd, and
printed and bound in Great Britain
by Biddles Ltd, Guildford and King's Lynn

A CIP record for this book is available
from the British Library

ISBN 0 7486 0527 4

# Contents

# Preface

It is no exaggeration to say that Scottish historical studies have been transformed in the last few decades, and in no area is this more evident than in the history of the Scottish Church, with the century of the Reformation a particularly favoured period. The fourth centenary of the Reformation Parliament in 1960 occasioned three important and influential works: Professor Gordon Donaldson's study on the nature of the emerging Protestant Church, the issues of the recently founded *Innes Review* reprinted as *Essays on the Scottish Reformation*, and Dr David Easson's meticulously referenced *Medieval Religious Houses: Scotland.*

Dr Easson's work provided for the first time a reliable list of monasteries with uncertain and supposed foundations excluded. A second edition by Professor Ian Cowan increased its value. Dr John Durkan's pioneering work on the Renaissance in Scotland and the universities, schools and hospitals (a term including every kind of caring institution) contained much on the involvement of the monasteries. The same is true of Professor Cowan's work on the administration of the late medieval Church. Dr Margaret Sanderson has investigated the administration of monastic lands and the widespread practice of feuing. My own work has been on the monks themselves, their superiors and their constitutional status.

Light has been shed on the monasteries by a further wide range of pioneering scholarly studies: on parishes, clergy and clerical officials, on universities and libraries, on saints and pilgrimages, on burghs and regalities, on farming and on taxation before and after 1560, and on churches and architecture. A fresh assessment of the monasteries in the light of the new available information was called for.

The six chapters of the present work are based, with very little change, on the six Rhind Lectures delivered in March 1993. To a large extent the lecture format determined the treatment of the material, and the aim here is not to present a full study of Scottish monasticism, or indeed of any particular feature of it. So much more could be said about the libraries, the buildings, the land economy and so on. Buildings, for instance, are twice considered briefly – not in their own right, but in the context of their upkeep demonstrating the morale of the monastic communities and of their magnificence adding to the prestige of the monasteries. The intention is rather to provide an over-all picture of these monastic communities, with emphasis on their lifestyle and ethos. Within this framework I hope to produce, at some future date, a fuller account of Scottish monastic life in the late Middle Ages insofar as the surviving sources permit.

The term 'monastery' here denotes the communities of monks and canons regular, while 'monk' in its generic sense includes canons regular as well as monks strictly so called. Canons regular are therefore included, but friars are not since the constitutional status of friars, their way of life, their ethos – in fact, almost everything about them – made them radically different from monks and regular canons. They were in no sense monks, and their inclusion would have resulted in two very diverse studies in uneasy juxtaposition. Including the nunneries would also have introduced a very dissimilar element.

Finally, I wish to thank the office-bearers of the Society of Antiquaries of Scotland, under whose auspices the lectures were given, for their help and kindness, which made the giving of the lectures a pleasant and memorable occasion. I am grateful also to the staff of the Scottish Record Office and of the National Library of Scotland for their unfailing courtesy and co-operation in making the printed and manuscript sources available, and to the Keeper of the Scottish Catholic Archives for allowing me such extensive use of the library and other facilities. Finally, I would like to thank Richard Fawcett for allowing me to use a selection of his photographs in this volume.

# 1

# *The Shaping of Scottish Monasticism*

Monasticism is basically a withdrawal from the everyday world for spiritual or religious reasons. It entails celibacy and a certain basic austerity. An early monastic writer put it succinctly: monks, he said, must flee from women and bishops.[1]

Christian monasticism began in the third century in the Egyptian desert, possibly under influence from the East.[2] It became a popular movement, with monks living either as hermits or in loose-knit communities, and in the fourth and fifth centuries men flocked to the Thebaid in upper Egypt to follow this way of life. The movement also spread west, reaching the Celtic lands in the sixth century. St Columba came to Iona in 563 and Celtic monks evangelised Europe from the sixth century on.

Monastic life also flourished in Italy but it was unco-ordinated, lacking in order and not always edifying. In the early sixth century St Benedict established several small monasteries at Monte Cassino and composed a Rule for them. He deliberately turned away from the individualistic and semi-eremitical lifestyle of the eastern groups, laying down instead an ordered and moderate life in community. His Rule envisaged no specific work or enterprise, and the chief activity was to be the communal choir office. The day was divided between prayer in public and private, *lectio* (reading aimed at spiritual formation) and work. The monks elected their superior, termed 'abbot', for life and owed him obedience, while he in turn was to consult them on important matters.

Benedict's Rule was gradually accepted almost universally, though there was still very great diversity between monasteries and no co-ordination. Various attempts made to standardise monastic observance, for intance under Charlemagne in the early ninth century, had only moderate success.

In 909–10 the abbey of Cluny in Burgundy was founded and embraced a strict way of life based on Benedict's Rule. The reform spread rapidly as other monasteries adopted it and new monasteries were founded. The Cluniac reform had two notable features: the lengthy and elaborate choir offices which filled the day, and the rigid centralisation which concentrated all real authority in the hands of the abbot of Cluny.

Cluniac monasteries achieved enormous success and influence. They were given the privilege of exemption from all Church authorities except the pope himself, and four Cluniac monks in fact became popes. The tenth and eleventh centuries have been called the Cluniac centuries, but Cluniac monasticism was to have only moderate relevance for Scotland.

There were reforms and new groupings elsewhere, for instance in Italy, though these never spread north. In Normandy a monastic revival was centred on the great abbey of Bec and involved two celebrated men from northern Italy, Lanfranc and Anselm. The revival crossed the Channel after the Norman Conquest in 1066; Lanfranc and Anselm both came to England and became in turn archbishop of Canterbury.[3] This revival too was to have limited relevance for Scotland.

What did affect Scotland powerfully and permanently was a remarkable monastic revival in France at the end of the eleventh century.[4] It was in fact to determine the nature and course of Scottish monasticism. Three men in particular opted for the strictest and most austere monastic life – they were St Bruno, St Bernard of Tiron and St Robert of Molesme.

In 1084 Bruno and six companions settled as hermits in the mountains of the Grande Chartreuse. Similar colonies multiplied and became the Carthusian order. (Carthusian comes from *Cartusia*, the Latin form of Chartreuse, while the English term 'charterhouse' for a Carthusian monastery is simply a corruption of Chartreuse.) Bruno based his way of life on the Rule of St Benedict, but with two very important differences. Where Benedict aimed at moderation, the Carthusian Rule was uncompromisingly austere, and where Benedict stressed the common life, Bruno stressed solitude and silence. Carthusians in fact were hermits living in community. Their relevance for Scotland was to come later.

Bernard of Tiron, a Benedictine monk, went to live with a colony of hermits in Brittany. Elected abbot of a Benedictine monastery, he resisted the claims of Cluny, then became a hermit once more. In 1109 he founded a monastery at Tiron near Chartres, which flourished and became the head of other monasteries, mostly in France. They were known as Tironensians.

The third man, Robert, left the monastery of Molesme with a group of monks in 1098 and settled in the woods at Cîteaux near Dijon. Their aim was to observe Benedict's Rule to the letter. After difficult beginnings, they began to expand rapidly, mainly through the influence of St Bernard of Clairvaux, who had joined them. They were known as Cistercians (from the Latin form of Cîteaux) and, because of their over-garment or cowl of unbleached wool, as White Monks.

It was a time of remarkable enthusiasm for monastic life, like upper Egypt 700 years before, with men flocking to join monasteries, so that there was even fear for the continuance of the human race! There was a desire to follow the traditional Rule of St Benedict, but in a radical and often literal way. Monks observing the Rule strictly were in great demand with both churchmen and secular authorities, and there was a fairly general reaction against Cluny's authoritarianism and elaborate choir offices.

Tiron was overshadowed by the Cistercian reform but both were very similar. Both aimed at simplicity, with the accretions in choir office removed and manual work restored, though where Cîteaux stressed agricultural work, Tiron emphasised arts and crafts. Both reforms were of the greatest importance for Scotland.

Equally important were the canons regular, that is, priests taking monastic vows and following the Rule of St Augustine.[5] They were the product of a long and complex process. From the earliest times, in various places, the clergy had tended to live together and in the early fourth century Augustine, who was a bishop, insisted on his clergy sharing a common life and wrote a Rule for them. *Canonici* (canons) came to mean clergy living in community.

Canons regular emerged as a definite monastic group in the mid-eleventh century, greatly stimulated by the Gregorian Reform with its stress on clerical celibacy. They followed no particular Rule, until gradually that of Augustine came to be universally accepted, as Benedict's was by monks. In fact the development of canons and monks had many similar features. As Augustine's Rule was brief and unspecific, the leading houses of canons compiled their own code of custom and discipline, based partly on Benedictine usages. As with Benedictines, houses of canons were not usually linked with each other; but again like Benedictines, some houses formed groups that were closely linked.

One such group was founded by St Norbert at Prémontré in northern France in 1120, with the aim of combining strict monastic life with pastoral work.[6] The life of these Premonstratensians (from the Latin form of Prémontré) comprised three main elements: the Rule of Augustine, Benedictine customs and considerable austerity. In fact Norbert, being a friend of Bernard of Clairvaux, took his ideals and organisation and even the colour of his habit from the Cistercians. These White Canons received papal approval in 1126, their statutes were finalised in the early 1130s and Norbert died in 1134. Both the unlinked Augustinians and the centralised Premonstratensians were important for Scotland.

For canons, clerical status, that is their priesthood, was of the essence and in this they differed from monks. The unavoidable tension in their life between their monastic ideals and their pastoral zeal was, however, resolved in favour of the former and in many ways they became indistinguishable from monks. The mainstream Benedictine monks and Augustinian canons wore black, the Cistercian monks and Premonstratensian canons wore white, and all were popularly known by the colour of their habit. And indeed the relationship of Black and White canons to each other was very like that of Black and White monks: the White monks and canons were more austere and more closely organised than their Black brethren.

The word *ordo* (order) causes some confusion. It was originally applied to all monks or canons as a body: *ordo monasticus*, *ordo canonicus*. It came to be applied to specific groups such as Cistercians and Premonstratensians, and also to Cluniacs and Tironensians despite their being seen as part of the Black Monk family.[7] Even today Benedictines, being uncentralised, are not technically speaking an order, while only the centralised groups of canons regular have survived.

That then was the situation in the early twelfth century. There was enormous monastic vitality and expansion, both of monks properly so called and of regular canons. Dom David Knowles has called the century 1050–1150 the monastic age par excellence.[8] At this very time St Benedict's Rule finally supplanted the Celtic monastic rules on the Continent,[9] and in Scotland itself the loose Celtic Church organisation was giving way to the more structured Continental organisation.[10] Rulers and bishops were strongly in favour of these new and fervent monastic groups. Celtic monasticism in Scotland lacked the vitality to resist, and they came flooding in.

The first Continental-style (as opposed to Celtic) monks arrived in Scotland about 1070 when, at Queen Margaret's request, Lanfranc sent three Benedictine monks from Canterbury to Dunfermline.[11] It was a very small beginning and Dunfermline was not a fully organised abbey until c. 1128. Already, by then, Tironensian monks had come to Selkirk in 1113, moving on to Kelso fifteen years later. This was the first foundation of any of the new monastic groups to arrive in Britain, and a few years later Earl David (later David I) visited Tiron and brought more monks back with him.

Augustinian canons also came: to Scone from Nostell in Yorkshire c. 1120, and to Holyrood in 1128 from Merton in Surrey. Cistercians came to Melrose in 1136 from Rievaulx in Yorkshire, and the first Premonstratensians arrived at Dryburgh from Alnwick in Northumberland in 1150.

There are two important points to be made. The first is the rapidity with which these new orders came to Scotland. Monks arrived from Tiron in 1113, only four years after Tiron itself was founded and while the founder Bernard was still alive. Cistercians arrived in 1136, which was long before the death of Bernard of Clairvaux in 1153. White Canons came only sixteen years after their statutes were drawn up and their founder Norbert died.

The second point is that, although all the houses except Kelso were founded from England, they were hardly English foundations. Black Monks came to Dunfermline in the aftermath of the Norman Conquest and the Norman stimulation of English monastic life, and indeed they were sent by Lanfranc, who had himself come from Normandy to England. Black Canons arrived not long after the foundation of their English mother-house, half a dozen years in the case of Scone and fourteen years in that of Holyrood. Melrose was founded only eight years after White Monks first crossed the Channel and only four years after their arrival at Rievaulx. It was the same with the White Canons at Dryburgh – seven years from their arrival in England and two to three years from the foundation of the mother-house.

These monks and canons – even if not actually French, and probably many were – were French-impelled. It was the great monastic expansion crossing the Channel and spreading north, a peaceful Norman Conquest of Scotland,[12] and in the case of the first new arrivals, the monks of Tiron, their first stopping-place was in Scotland.

And not only did the new groups come quickly to Scotland, they spread with great rapidity once they arrived. In the period 1113–1230, slightly over a century, there were founded thirty important monasteries belonging to seven monastic groups, with over a dozen less important foundations. It was an expansion which must bear comparison with any monastic revival anywhere.

Mainline Benedictines achieved no notable expansion, for the new orders were now in the van. Three priories were founded which remained dependent on their mother-house: Coldingham on Durham, Urquhart (Moray) on Dunfermline, Isle of May on Reading. The one new abbey, Iona, was founded c. 1203 by the Lord of the Isles, probably from Ireland.[13]

Tironensians on the other hand multiplied by four at least. Kelso founded a dependent priory at Lesmagahow in 1144 and was no doubt the main founder of three other abbeys in the years 1162–91: Kilwinning, Arbroath, Lindores.

Augustinians achieved notable expansion. Two abbeys were founded from northern France: Jedburgh from Beauvais c. 1138 and Cambuskenneth from Arrouaise c. 1140. Arrouaise was like Prémontré in being the head of a centralised group. The canons at St Andrews, founded from Scone in 1144, formed the cathedral chapter.[14] Abbeys were established at Inchcolm c. 1153 and at Inchaffray in 1200, while Jedburgh, St Andrews and Holyrood also had dependent priories. Black Canons had settled in some of the most important places in Scotland.

The most dramatic increase was that of the Cistercians. In 1140, after only four years, Melrose founded Newbattle and not much later established Kinloss and Holmcultram (Cumbria). Rievaulx made a second foundation at Dundrennan. The general chapter at Cîteaux forbade new foundations in the 1150s but the tide could not be stemmed. Melrose founded two more houses at Coupar Angus and Balmerino; Kinloss established two at Culross and Deer; Dundrennan founded Glenluce; Saddell in Kintyre was founded from Ireland. There were now ten Cistercian abbeys in Scotland.

Five more Premonstratensian houses were established: Soulseat, Whithorn, Tongland and Holywood in the South-West and Fearn in the eastern Highlands. The canons at Whithorn formed the cathedral chapter. Somewhat surprisingly, for the fortunes of Cluny had peaked some time before, a Cluniac house was founded at Paisley in 1169. Even more surprisingly, it became an abbey in 1219.

Finally, in 1230–1, three Valliscaulian priories were established at Pluscarden, Beauly and Ardchattan. This was a new order recognised by Rome in 1205. The title Valliscaulian comes from the Latinised form of Val des Choux in Burgundy, where the order was founded, and indeed these priories were the only houses of the order outwith France. By c. 1230 there were thus in Scotland thirty important monasteries: twenty-eight abbeys and two cathedral priories, and that was in addition to a fair number of priories and dependent priories.

A word of explanation should be given on priors and priories. In the Rule of St Benedict the head of a monastery was an abbot. Gradually, however, monasteries came to have a second-in-command, termed a prior. Gradually, too, a monastery headed by an abbot and termed an abbey acquired a certain status, while a lesser monastery was a priory with a prior at its head. To use modern terminology, a claustral prior was second-in-command in an abbey, while a conventual prior was superior in a priory.

There were four reasons for a monastery being a priory:

1. It had not achieved independence of the mother-house. In traditional language, the umbilical cord had not been cut.

2. It had obtained independence but had not graduated to abbatial status. This could be temporary, for instance at Scone founded c. 1120 and made an abbey c. 1164, or it could be permanent. Houses of White Monks and Canons, however, were usually abbeys from the outset.
3. Houses of Carthusians and Valliscaulians (founded by a Carthusian) were never abbeys, and Carthusians at least did not want permanent abbots but removable priors.
4. Cathedral monasteries were always priories. The reason was historical. Originally the bishop was a monk and abbot of the monastery attached to his cathedral. When the bishop was no longer a monk, the former second-in-command became head of the autonomous monastery but retained the title of prior, though in fact a cathedral prior was more important than most abbots.[15]

The monastic expansion in Scotland was not due simply to monks having to find a new home for themselves, for influential patrons wished them to come. Notable men invited them, endowed them handsomely, and perhaps saw to the building of their new home. The most prolific founders were the kings, particularly David I (1124–53), though the Lord of the Isles, lords of Galloway and earls and bishops were also founders.

While the expansion in Scotland must be among the most impressive in the annals of monasticism, the part played by David I was exceptional, and he surely deserves to rank among the greatest monastic founders of any period or country. This was to have important consequences in the sixteenth century. When James I described his ancestor David as 'ane sair sanct for the Croune',[16] it was not merely a wry remark. The Scottish kings considered that the benefactions of their forebears not only gave them rights and privileges but also justified their taking fairly strong-arm measures, including getting some of their money back.

The scope of the present study can now be precisely defined. It comprises those monasteries that were a permanent fixed abode for monks or regular canons, who made their profession (that is, took their vows) for that house, and where the superior held office for life. Dependent priories are, however, included with the parent house, which controlled them. Not included are the nunneries, the Trinitarians, though they were like canons regular in some ways, or the Gilbertines. The latter were in Scotland for a very short time and were really a women's order with men brought in to provide some necessary help. Augustinians not fulfilling the above criteria are excluded, for instance those in hospitals such as Soutra or the unknown quantity of clerics living together and following Augustine's Rule.

In the thirteenth, fourteenth and fifteenth centuries, Scotland and its monasteries underwent great changes. One need only think of the coming of the friars and the rise of the universities. Here, however, only two interrelated episodes need be considered: the wars with England and the Great Schism. English invasions brought much destruction to Scottish monasteries, and naturally links between Scottish dependent priories and their mother-houses in England were severed. In those wars too, Scotland was the ally of France and in the Great Schism adhered to the Avignon pope, and well over half the Scottish monasteries had links with France. As a result the Schism caused little disruption to Scottish monasticism, not a fraction of that suffered by monasteries in England.[17] It is also very possible that Scottish monasteries were a factor in preserving and fostering Franco-Scottish sentiment.

In those three centuries only one new monastic order came to Scotland, the Carthusians. James I, having returned to Scotland in 1424, was zealous for monastic reform and was also surely aware of the great expansion of Carthusians in England over the previous decades.[18] He therefore almost at once set about founding a monastery for these most austere monks at Perth. Charterhouses, however, do not just grow, for there is strict uniformity and control by the Grande Chartreuse over the meticulously regulated way of life and thus necessarily over the buildings and material arrangements. Each monk lives for most of the day in a hermitage opening off the main cloister, while laybrothers deal with the material arrangements. Perth charterhouse came quickly into being and the first community, including at least one Scot, arrived from the Continent. The second prior was a Scot and Scottish recruits began at once to enter the noviciate.[19]

Other changes over the three centuries were slight. Pluscarden (Valliscaulian) was made a Benedictine dependent priory of Dunfermline in place of Urquhart, which was suppressed. A second Cluniac abbey was founded at Crossraguel. One new Cistercian abbey was founded, Sweetheart or New Abbey, and Saddell was suppressed. Several Augustinian priories were founded, while the Benedictine priory on the Isle of May ended up as Augustinian and at Pittenweem on the mainland.

Something should be said about the rise and decline of Kelso. In its early days it achieved remarkable importance. Its first two abbots were promoted to be abbots of Tiron itself, and in 1165 Rome granted to the abbot of Kelso the privilege of *pontificalia* (use of mitre, crozier and other insignia of bishops). This was the first grant of its kind in Scotland and with it Rome conferred exemption from the jurisdiction of the local bishop and of Tiron. Kelso henceforth was subject directly to Rome with no intermediary. Roman documents refer to Kelso as *filia specialis Sanctae Sedis* (special daughter of the Holy See), a title which does not imply Rome's special affection for Kelso but rather that Rome supplied the intermediate level of jurisdiction which was lacking. In 1176 the abbot of Kelso disputed precedence with the abbot of Tiron, no doubt on the strength of this exemption.[20] It is therefore most unlikely that Kelso's three daughter-houses at Kilwinning, Arbroath and Lindores would have had any direct connection with Tiron and there seems to be no evidence of further links between Scotland and Tiron. As for Kelso itself, it was surpassed in wealth and prestige by Arbroath; then in the early fifteenth century the prior of St Andrews replaced the abbot of Kelso as the prelate taking first place among the monastic superiors.[21]

As the sixteenth century dawned, the Scottish monastic scene differed in various ways from that in any other country. So many houses were Cistercian or Augustinian rather than Benedictine or Cluniac. There were important abbeys of Tironensian origin, which was rare outside France, even if this was by now a matter of history rather than current relevance. The only Valliscaulian houses outside France were in Scotland. Cathedral chapters of canons regular were uncommon,[22] yet there were two in Scotland. Rarer still were Cluniac houses with abbatial status, yet both the Scottish houses were abbeys. And not only was Scottish monasticism unique in its mix of orders and houses, but many developments and factors in Scotland were unlike those in any other country.

# MAPS

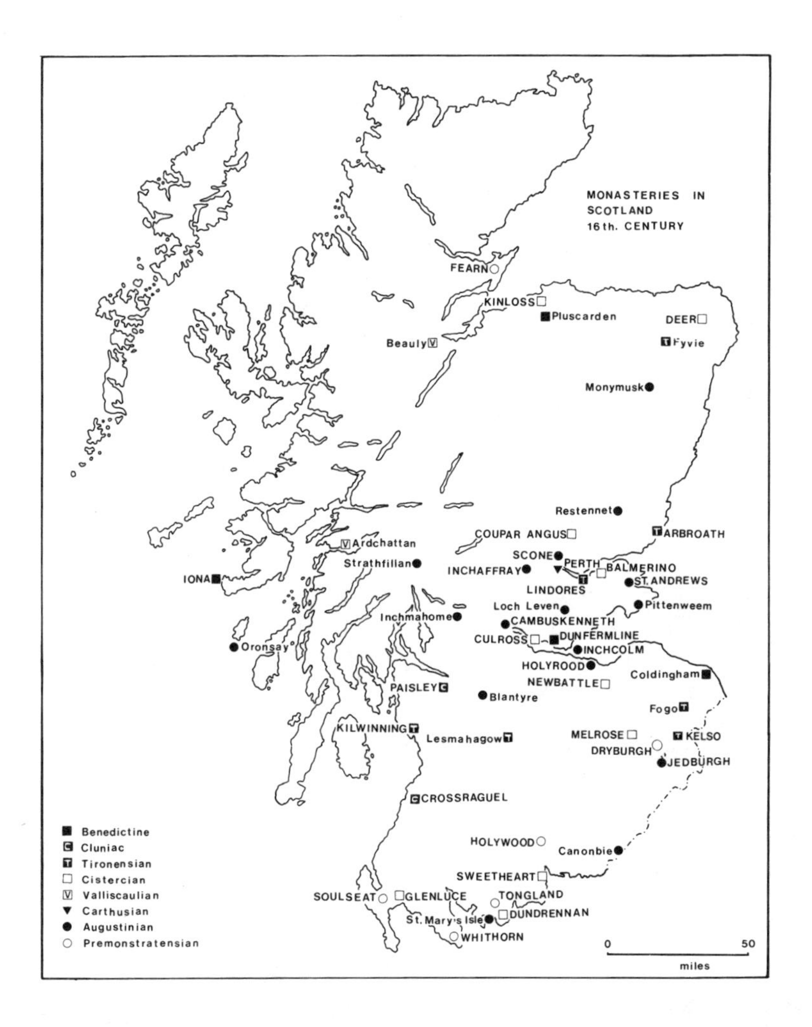
MONASTERIES IN SCOTLAND 16th. CENTURY
FEARN
KINLOSS
Pluscarden
DEER
Fyvie
Beauly
Monymusk
Restennet
ARBROATH
COUPAR ANGUS
Ardchattan
SCONE
PERTH
BALMERINO
Strathfillan
INCHAFFRAY
IONA
LINDORES
ST. ANDREWS
Loch Leven
Pittenweem
Inchmahome
CAMBUSKENNETH
CULROSS
DUNFERMLINE
INCHCOLM
Oronsay
HOLYROOD
NEWBATTLE
Coldingham
PAISLEY
Blantyre
Fogo
KILWINNING
Lesmahagow
MELROSE
KELSO
DRYBURGH
JEDBURGH
CROSSRAGUEL
HOLYWOOD
Canonbie
SWEETHEART
SOULSEAT
GLENLUCE
TONGLAND
St. Mary's Isle
DUNDRENNAN
WHITHORN
Benedictine
Cluniac
Tironensian
Cistercian
Valliscaulian
Carthusian
Augustinian
Premonstratensian
0
50
miles

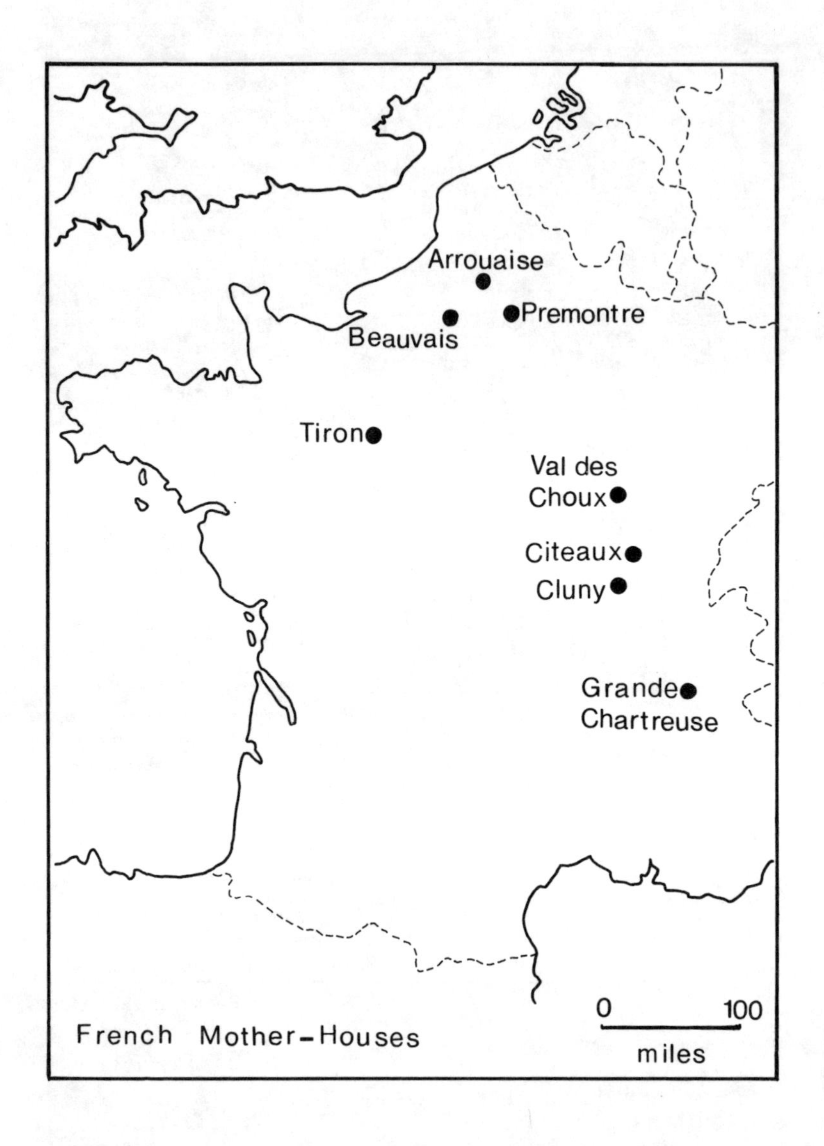
Arrouaise
Premontre
Beauvais
Tiron
Val des Choux
Citeaux
Cluny
Grande Chartreuse
0
100
miles
French Mother-Houses

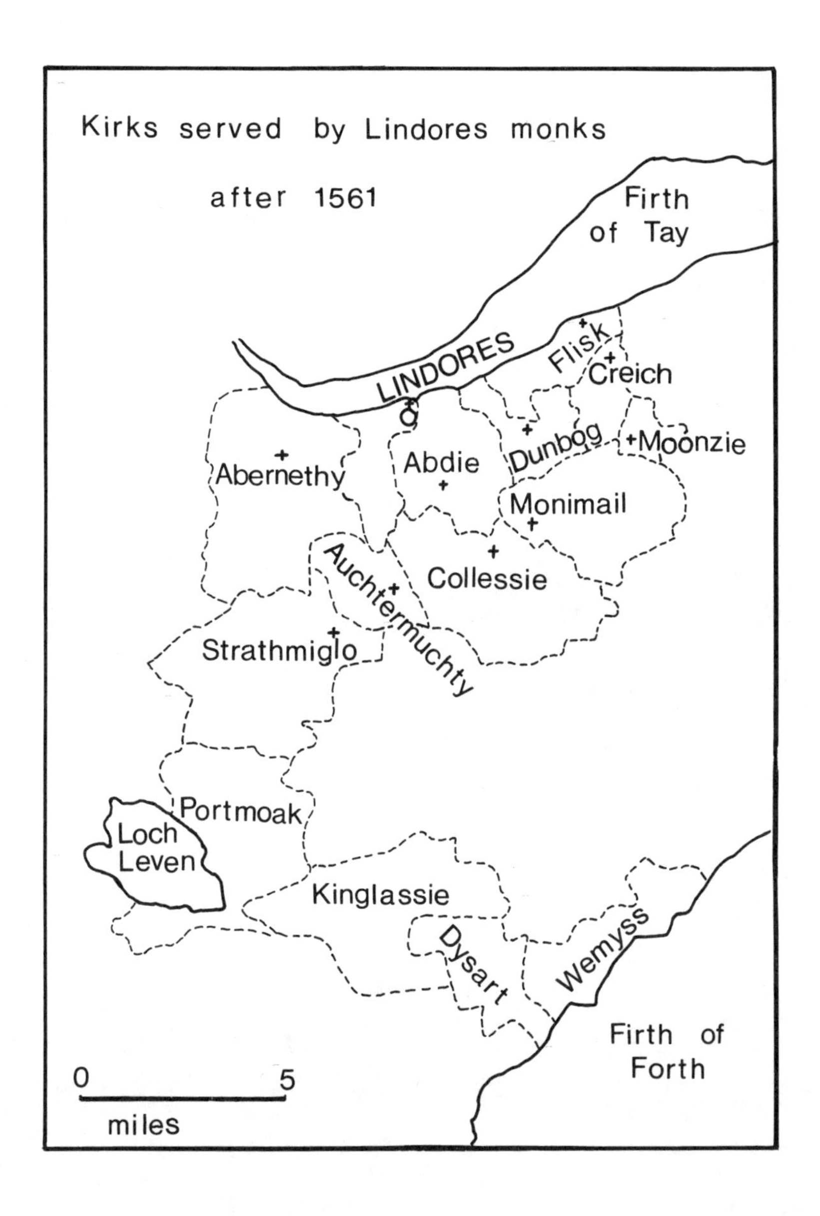
Kirks served by Lindores monks
after 1561
Firth of Tay
LINDORES
Flisk
Creich
Dunbog
Moonzie
Abernethy
Abdie
Monimail
Auchtermuchty
Collessie
Strathmiglo
Portmoak
Loch Leven
Kinglassie
Dysart
Wemyss
Firth of Forth
0
5
miles

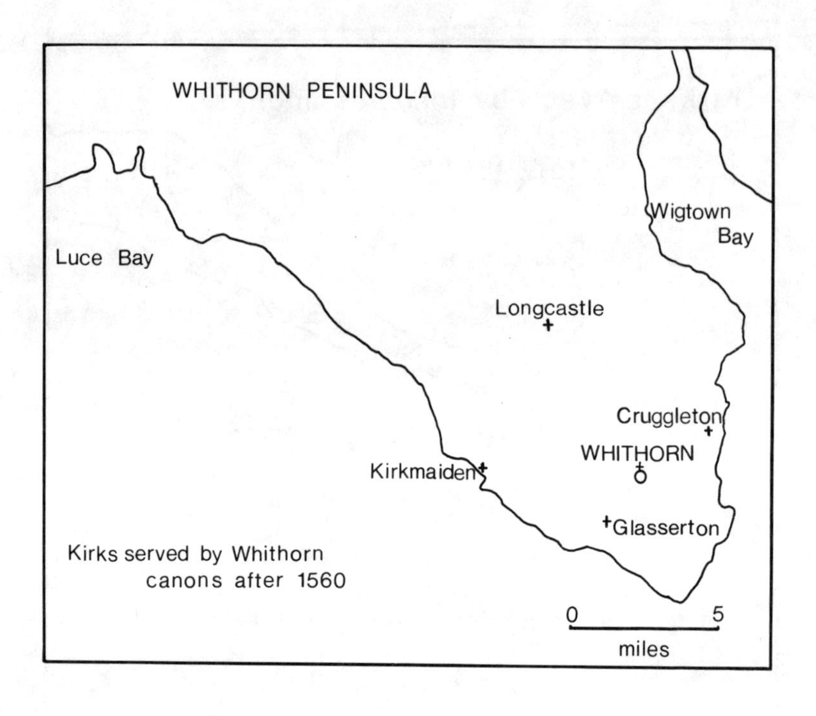
WHITHORN PENINSULA
Luce Bay
Wigtown Bay
Longcastle
Cruggleton
WHITHORN
Kirkmaiden
Glasserton
Kirks served by Whithorn canons after 1560
0
5
miles

## NOTES

1. Dickinson, *Origins*, p. 10.
2. For a general survey of monasticism from its origins to c. 1100, see Cousin, *Précis*, pp. 27–254; Knowles, *Christian Monasticism*, pp. 9–61.
3. Knowles, *Monastic Order*, pp. 31–144.
4. Cousin, *Précis*, pp. 255–95; Knowles, *Christian Monasticism*, pp. 62–97; Knowles, *Monastic Order*, pp. 191–226. Informative articles on individuals and groups are to be found in *Catholic Encyclopedia*, *New Catholic Encyclopedia*, *DHGE* and *DSCHT*.
5. Dickinson, *Origins*, pp. 1–90.
6. Colvin, *White Canons*, pp. 1–26.
7. Dickinson, *Origins*, pp. 79, 162. Knowles entitles his book *The Monastic Order*.
8. Knowles, *Christian Monasticism*, p. 77.
9. Dilworth, *Scots in Franconia*, pp. 11–12.
10. G. Donaldson, *Scotland: Church and Nation through Sixteen Centuries* (London 1960), pp. 14–21.
11. For developments in Scotland see *MRHS*, passim; Barrow, *Kingdom of Scots*, pp. 165–211. Other references are supplementary.
12. Cruden, *Medieval Churches*, pp. 21–147, especially 21, 63.
13. See pp. 59–60 below.
14. For developments at St Andrews see Barrow, *Kingdom of Scots*, pp. 212–32.
15. Dilworth, 'Augustinian Chapter', pp. 121–31.
16. Boece/Bellenden, *The Chronicles of Scotland*, ii (STS 1941), p. 185.
17. Knowles, *Religious Orders*, ii, pp. 167–70.
18. *ibid.*, pp. 129–38.
19. Beckett, 'Perth Charterhouse', pp. 1–74, especially pp. 31–32, 35; Thompson, *Carthusian Order*, pp. 246–8; J. Ferguson, 'The Carthusian Order in Scotland', *TSES* iii (1909–12), pp. 179–92.
20. *Kelso Lib.*, pp. vii–ix; nos 438–9, 443, 447, 460–1, 467.
21. *Ibid.*, xli; *Joannis de Fordun Scotichronicon cum Supplementis … Walteri Boweri* (Edinburgh, 1759), Lib. VI, Cap. 49.
22. Backmund, 'Premonstratensian Order', p. 39; Colvin, *White Canons*, p. 363.

# 2

# *Monastic Prelates*

Chapter 64 of the Rule of St Benedict gives excellent spiritual advice on choosing an abbot but is less helpful on the practical side. The abbot was to be the man chosen by the whole community or even by the smaller but wiser part of it, and if the monks chose badly the local bishop and others were to step in and rectify matters.

But who was to decide which group was wiser, and how would the other group be persuaded that they were less wise? And what if it was not a simple choice between black and white? A system therefore developed, whereby in one way or another the election was determined by a majority vote, while some person from outside, for instance the local bishop or the abbot of the mother-house, presided over the election and confirmed it.

In the middle ages there were three modes of election:

1. *Via Spiritus Sancti* (way of the Holy Spirit): a name was said aloud and there was either acclamation or consenting silence.
2. *Via compromissi* (way of compromise): a person or persons were chosen, usually an odd number to avoid a split decision, and it was agreed that their choice would be accepted.
3. *Via scrutinii* (way of scrutiny): a few monks were chosen and went aside; each declared his choice, then each of the other monks came singly and told them his choice. A notary recorded each vote. A secret ballot seems to have been unknown in the Middle Ages.

When the person elected accepted his election, the bells were rung, the monks processed to the church singing the *Te Deum*, and the election was publicly announced. He later received the abbatial blessing from the bishop. If the person elected was not eligible, for instance if he was under the canonical age or of illegitimate birth or not a monk, he was postulated, which meant that higher authority had to permit his election.

Detailed accounts of each form of election have survived, for example the way of the Holy Spirit at Cambuskenneth in 1336, the way of compromise at Arbroath in 1484, the way of scrutiny at St Andrews in 1417. On reading the accounts, one is left with the distinct impression that, not unnaturally, much had been decided beforehand.[1] Election by the monks was satisfactory if the abbot was simply to be the spiritual father of his community. It was quite inadequate if the monastery was wealthy and the abbatial office was one of prestige and power, and if the abbot was a prelate with mitre and crozier and likely to be used by the king for important affairs of state, which was in fact the case in Scotland.

Elections were gradually taken out of the monks' hands.[2] Rome began to reserve appointments of abbots to its own jurisdiction; the technical term for this kind of appointment was provision. In 1265, for instance, the appointment was reserved if the vacancy arose from the death of the existing prelate at Rome or within two days' journey from Rome. There were further categories, for example if the vacancy arose through an abbot being promoted (e.g. being made a bishop) by Rome, or if he had resigned his abbacy into the hands of the pope or a papal legate.[3] Some benefices were reserved if they fell vacant in certain months of the year and not in others.[4] It was a recipe for chaos.

In preparation of the Holy Year of 1350, the holy see reserved to itself the appointment to the benefice of anyone dying while on pilgrimage to Rome, whether he died at Rome or on the journey there or back. The abbot of Dunfermline having died during his pilgrimage, the community elected a new abbot, who was duly confirmed in office and received the abbatial blessing. Then, in 1351, the pope (in Avignon at this time) stepped in and provided someone else as abbot.[5] By the mid-fifteenth century, however, Roman provision was needed for all monasteries of any importance.

Usually Rome provided the person who had already been elected, as for instance after the election at St Andrews in 1417 mentioned above,[6] and he then held office in virtue of his provision. Sometimes, as at Dunfermline in 1351, provision was made of a monk or canon regular other than the one elected. Gradually, however, it became more common to provide one who was not already a monk, in which case he had to assume the monastic habit and make his profession, that is, take the monastic vows.

Provisions of non-monks increased greatly during the Great Schism (1378–1417) as both Rome and Avignon used the power of provision to gain and reward supporters. Monastic prelacies were a target for the ambitious and the covetous, with papal provision intended to act as a check but in fact stimulating the process. The Roman court became a market, whither ambitious clerics came to canvass on the spot, while Rome needed the fees payable by the successful candidates. Secular rulers could not permit this, for not only did they lose their power of patronage but the abbots who were provided, perhaps unacceptable to them, held positions of importance and often sat in parliament or council. In consequence legislation was passed against clerics getting preferment in Rome and inevitably there was confrontation between Rome and the rulers. Eventually a measure of agreement was reached.[7]

A further development was to provide a non-monk but without imposing on him the monastic obligations of wearing the habit and taking vows. In other words he remained a non-monk and held office as a commendator, meaning that he was simply entrusted with the duties of a monastic superior. The practice of commendation was in fact much older than provision. As early as the sixth century, a person not the legal holder of an ecclesiastical office could be put in to do the duties. He was really an administrator and he received the emolument attached to the office. Increasingly, however, the appointment was made for life and for the benefit of the commendator rather than of the institution. Increasingly, too, commendation was confined to monastic prelacies.

Commendation not only allowed a non-monk to be appointed to a monastic benefice, but it also evaded the laws against pluralism, the holding of incompatible benefices, that is positions to which a revenue was attached. For instance, being a bishop in one place was clearly incompatible with being an abbot somewhere else, but a bishop could in law hold an abbacy as a commendator. There was a legal principle that only one benefice could be held by right, but additional ones could be held as commends.

The modern reader runs a danger here of misunderstanding the status of some abbots. The Latin word *titulus* (title) meant being entitled to a benefice, having it by right; its opposite, *commenda*, meant being entrusted with it as an administrator. A titular abbot was thus a monk and a real abbot, whereas titular nowadays implies an empty title without substance.[8]

As commendation became more widespread its effect on monastic life, particularly in the Mediterranean countries, was disastrous. France suffered less, but commendation became the accepted system and from 1438 on the king controlled appointments to abbacies. In England, on the other hand, commendation was almost unknown. Scotland followed the pattern of the Continent, though with significant differences. Every provision to Scottish monasteries during the Great Schism was of a monk, as was almost every provision for fifty years after. Monks and regular canons began, however, to petition Rome for prelacies for themselves, either as superior of their own monastery or of another monastery of the same order or even of another though similar order, often giving reasons why the present incumbent should be deposed.[9] Dr Coulton, commenting on this, declares it was the era of *Official Recognition of the Common Informer* (italics his).[10] 'Unscrupulous Claimant' would be more accurate. It was a development completely opposed to the spirit of monasticism and the Rule of St Benedict, and the reality was no doubt worse than the documents show, for only the successful petitions are known to us.

Rome on its side began to provide non-monks. The first was perhaps Alexander Fraser, vicar of Abertarff, made prior of Beauly in 1430. In 1449 Richard Guthrie, of Brechin diocese, was provided to Arbroath, and thereafter provision of non-monks became more common. It also became more common to grant a temporary commend, usually of six months to two years, to such a person: he would thus have jurisdiction and enjoy the prelatial revenues at once, although not obliged to become a monk until his commend ended. The first perpetual commendator was Bishop James Kennedy, provided to Scone in 1439. In fact a bishop could only be a commendator, for his episcopal office precluded his becoming a monk. A few other commendations to bishops followed, usually in particular circumstances, and gradually bishop-commendators became more common. By 1513, the year of the battle of Flodden, it was quite usual for secular (that is, not monastic) clerics to become abbots and for bishops to become commendators.

The Scottish rulers did not stand idly by. Sometimes the Crown intervened in a monastic election or provision, and laws were enacted against seeking provision or commendation in Rome. Finally, in 1487, an agreement with the pope was reached. The king received an indult (that is, a favour) whereby there would be an eight-month delay in provision to major benefices, which included most monasteries of any importance. Rome would await the king's nomination and would give provision to the nominee, and during the vacancy the revenues of the benefice would go to the king.[11]

After the death of so many churchmen at Flodden a new type of commendator appeared in Scotland – one who, although not a bishop, was granted a permanent commend. Before describing the monastic superiors between Flodden and the Reformation Parliament in 1560, however, a word should be said about the sources. No monastic archive has survived, though monastic documents (cartularies, for instance) have survived in isolation. Documents such as charters have remained with the families who gained possession of monastic land.[12] Roman records are available, though not much concerning the period after 1513 has been printed. Finally there are the Scottish public records and miscellaneous documents. To follow the developments and discern the patterns, to see the kind of person who became abbot, one has to put isolated items together.

A second preliminary is to clear the ground by seeing which monasteries were affected. Most of the small dependent priories had no community; the prior was there alone and it hardly matters who he was or how he was appointed. These were the cell of Arbroath at Fyvie and that of Kelso at Fogo, and the Augustinian priories of Loch Leven, Blantyre, Canonbie, Restenneth and Trail. Two Augustinian priories, Strathfillan and Oronsay, were verging on having no community. Again, it hardly mattered who was prior. Lesmahagow had a community, in the 1550s at least, but was linked with Kelso.

As for the Perth charterhouse, the prior was appointed and removed by the Carthusian general chapter and Rome did not intervene. Three other monasteries were withdrawn from the struggle. Iona Abbey was joined to the see of the Isles in 1498–9, to be its cathedral and probably also its cathedral chapter. This was because, with the hostilities between Scotland and England, the see of Sodor was necessarily divided into two, and its former cathedral was on the Isle of Man.[13] Tongland likewise was joined to the diocese of Galloway in 1530, and Beauly was placed under Kinloss in 1531. That left thirty-five houses, including all the important ones: three Black Benedictine, two Cluniac, four ex-Tironensian, ten Cistercian, one Valliscaulian, and among the canons ten Augustinian and five Premonstratensian.[14]

The more important prelacies were provided in consistory, that is, a meeting of cardinals. We have a fascinating glimpse behind the scenes in 1517 when a successor was being provided to replace the abbot of Arbroath, who had been killed at Flodden. There were three candidates: Andrew Forman (archbishop of St Andrews), James Beaton (archbishop of Glasgow) and James Stewart, a natural son of James IV. Three documents were produced, in which Forman renounced all claim to the abbacy, Stewart resigned Arbroath in favour of Beaton but was given a pension of £1,000 yearly from Arbroath revenues, and Beaton consented to the pension. Three Scots clerics in Rome were sworn in and testified to the authenticity of the documents, the character of the candidates and various details about Arbroath.

Simultaneously there was a consistorial process for providing Thomas Ker to Kelso. It was very similar – Scots clerics swore to details about Kelso, while Forman was again a candidate.[15] Both processes were typical in many ways. Important churchmen were adding great abbeys to the honours and revenues they already enjoyed, and the unsuccessful claimants were receiving massive compensation. In the event Forman was allowed to hold Dunfermline as well as his archbishopric;[16] while in Stewart's case – he was earl of Moray, described in the papal document as 16 or 17 years old, and his later career was not in the Church – the Crown was given a massive subsidy from church revenues to support a royal bastard.[17]

A heavy fee, called 'common services' and amounting to about a third of the annual revenues, was payable to Rome for consistorial provision.

Often a Continental banker loaned the money and had to be repaid with interest. At every provision numerous bulls were issued, which went some way to justify the large fee.[18] Seven have survived of those issued when John Hamilton was appointed to Arbroath in 1551, and eight issued for David Erskine, appointed to Dryburgh in 1556. They were to the new prelate, the sovereign, the bishop of the diocese, the convent (community), the vassals, the commissioners appointed to receive the oath of loyalty to the Holy See; another bull absolved from excommunication, whether it was needed or not.[19]

These two were commendators. When the non-monk provided was to take the habit, a papal mandate was sent to the community, as for instance when Robert Cairncross became abbot of Holyrood in 1528.[20] The text read (in translation):

> The Holy See ought to support the pious resolve of those wishing to live a religious life for the praise of God's name. As our beloved son, Robert Cairncross, priest of Glasgow diocese, wishes to produce the fruit of a better life in the religious habit together with the community of Holyrood, we want to foster him in his praiseworthy resolve ... therefore, if he is suitable, receive him as a brother, give him the religious habit and receive his religious vows.

One is perfectly justified in viewing such texts cynically, for the motives were usually anything but spiritual. Cairncross had three children legitimated only nine years later.[21] It is more realistic, however, to regard the texts as legal formulae rather than nauseating hypocrisy. At Pittenweem, a lesser monastery, the archbishop subdelegated the subprior to give the habit to the newly appointed prior.[22]

The papal indult of 1487, referred to earlier, was not binding on the pope's successor. After Flodden Leo X did not wait eight months for royal nominations but made his own appointments. He then changed course and in 1519 confirmed the indult. In 1526 the Scottish parliament made it treason to assume a prelacy without royal nomination and papal provision, then in 1535 Paul III admitted the king's right (no longer merely a concession) of nomination and extended the period of grace from eight to twelve months, with the Crown drawing the revenues in the interval. Nevertheless Rome would always try to increase its power in times of difficulty arising from royal minority or from unrest, as did all the interested parties: the local lords, the communities themselves and Henry VIII from south of the border.[23]

After Flodden the country was in an unsettled condition and at Whithorn in 1516 there were rival candidates. The Pope's choice was an Italian cardinal, while Governor Albany nominated Alexander Stewart, his own illegitimate half-brother. The impasse lasted until 1520, when a second nominee of Albany bought off the other two.[24] Much the same happened at Glenluce in 1516 but in this case with three candidates: another Italian cardinal, the pope's choice; the bishop of Lismore, Albany's nominee; and a monk of Glenluce, elected by the community and confirmed by the abbot of Cîteaux. Albany's nominee was successful and the monk was imprisoned.[25] In 1518 the canons of both Scone and Dryburgh elected their own abbot. Action was taken against Scone in the privy council, while at Dryburgh the whole community was put to the horn (declared outlaw) and ordered to be warded in St Andrews castle (though this probably did not actually happen).[26]

In 1524 the monks of Coupar Angus elected a monk as abbot, whom the abbot of Melrose confirmed in the name of Cîteaux. There were two other candidates. The Crown chose one of these, Donald Campbell, brother of the earl of Argyll, and obliged the abbot of Melrose to declare the monk's election quashed and have the royal nominee elected, while the privy council threatened to disperse the community unless it obeyed.[27] In fact a monastic community could not win against the papal indult to the king, the law of Scotland and the state's powers of compulsion.

Nevertheless, when the abbot of Newbattle died in 1529, the community at once elected one of their own number. James V then ordered them to elect James Haswell, his elemosinar. The subprior summoned the monastic chapter, declared the previous election quashed and informed Rome that Haswell had been postulated *via Spiritus Sancti*. No doubt technically he had been, with no voice raised in objection when his name was uttered.[28] The motives of the Crown in these appointments were very often financial – paying royal officials, rewarding for services rendered, bestowing favours.

If a bishop was given an abbacy he was of necessity a commendator, for his status as a ruling bishop, as we have seen, precluded his becoming a monk. The same is true of the occasional foreign cardinal, from the ineffective provision of one to Dunfermline in 1491 to the equally ineffective appointment of the queen dowager's brother, the Cardinal of Guise, to Melrose and Kelso in 1559.[29] This was so also for the holder of a lesser benefice if he retained it; George Durie, for instance, remained archdeacon of St Andrews and thus was commendator of Dunfermline.[30] If a regular abbot became a bishop but remained at the head of his monastery, he was now necessarily a commendator. Such were George Hepburn, abbot of Arbroath, made bishop of the Isles in 1511; Robert Reid, abbot of Kinloss, made bishop of Orkney in 1541; John Hamilton, abbot of Paisley, made bishop of Dunkeld in 1544. Patrick Hepburn, Augustinian prior of St Andrews, became in 1538 bishop of Moray and commendator of Scone. The case of Farquhar MacLean is even clearer, for in 1530 he became bishop of the Isles and commendator of Iona, the monastery where he had been until then a simple monk.[31]

A man belonging to a different monastic order could only be a commendator. George Crichton, Benedictine abbot of Dunfermline, became commendator of Augustinian Holyrood in 1500. A canon of St Andrews was made commendator of Beauly (Valliscaulian) in 1529. William Kennedy, abbot of Crossraguel (Cluniac), was simultaneously commendator of Holywood (Premonstratensian).[32]

It has already been said that a non-monk provided to an abbacy was often given a temporary commend – two years became the usual period – before being obliged to take the monastic habit. A worse abuse came into being: a child being given a commend until he was 22, apparently the minimum age for being blessed as a regular abbot. Such were John Hamilton, natural son of the earl of Arran, given Paisley as a commend in 1525 when aged about 14; James Stewart, given Inchcolm in 1544; and James Gordon, appointed to Glenluce in 1547. Even worse was to follow, when boys of tender years were made commendators for life. In 1534–41 four bastard sons of James V were made commendators of five important monasteries – Kelso, Melrose, Holyrood, Coldingham and St Andrews. Their ages can be gauged from their father's year of birth, 1512, and during this long minority the Crown received the abbatial revenues.[33] Two young sons of Châtelherault were given commends: one received Inchaffray, then Arbroath; the other was given Paisley.[34] The higher the social rank and the more important the office of state, the more likely was the person appointed to be a commendator rather than a regular abbot, though in a handful of cases a person of noble rank was a genuine monk.[35]

One last development needs to be outlined. This was *resignatio in favorem*, resigning in favour of a designated person, which became prevalent at the beginning of the sixteenth century. It meant in practice that there was no vacancy, for a deal had been made over the succession, with the Scottish Crown and Rome both concurring. The king gave leave, the abbot tendered his resignation to Rome; Rome accepted it and provided the new abbot. The old abbot got a pension from the revenues and also the right of regress, that is, of repossession if the new abbot died or resigned.[36] Often the new abbot was a nephew of the old one, and the monastery remained with the family.

There was a refinement of this – *resignatio cum retentione*, resigning the abbacy but holding on to it. The resigning abbot stayed in office, but the succession was fixed; the new abbot, especially if he was a nephew, was more or less the heir and sometimes the two ruled together. Beatons succeeded each other at Melrose, Dunfermline and Arbroath, as did Hamiltons at Paisley, Colvilles at Culross, Humes at Jedburgh.[37] All this was worlds away from the fervent, austere monks of the twelfth century electing one of their number as their spiritual leader.

And yet, in spite of everything, the system was not altogether bad. There were some redeeming features. It was not always harmful to monastic life, and the trends were not invariably in one direction. No layman was ever a commendator in Scotland; in fact the evidence is overwhelming that every commendator had to be in major orders, which made it impossible for him to contract a valid marriage. Adam Blackadder, commendator of Coldingham in the 1530s, petitioned Rome for a dispensation from taking major orders. Three times he was granted a two-years' postponement and finally a period of six months only.

Every commendator who married resigned his commend, for instance James Johnston at Soulseat in the 1530s. When the heir to the Erskine earldom was killed at Pinkie, the second-eldest son resigned his commend of Dryburgh in order to take his place; when he in turn died, the third-eldest resigned Dryburgh, for he was now the heir. He married and was later the Regent Mar. Many commendators married after the Reformation settlement of 1560, but not before. This was the case with William Colville (Culross), James Stewart (Inchcolm) and even James V's natural sons: Robert (Holyrood), John (Coldingham) and James (St Andrews). This James (later the Regent Moray) in fact was in major orders, being a deacon, and was regarded as a cleric by his half-sister, Queen Mary.

The only man who retained a commend although married was Mark Ker at Newbattle, who was certainly a cleric, for he was repledged to a church court when in trouble with the law. Provided to Newbattle as a temporary commendator, later to take the habit, he obtained a dispensation from this obligation from the legate *a latere* to the Emperor. Though obtained without authorisation from Rome and thus almost certainly invalid in law, the dispensation removed an obligation (to become a monk) incompatible with marriage.[38] For a married man to be a commendator was not impossible but had never been permitted by Rome in Scotland.

Provision of non-monks was sometimes actually of benefit to monasteries. Two such men, Alexander Myln at Cambuskenneth and Robert Reid at Kinloss, were notable restorers of monastic life. Being a monk evidently meant something to Myln, for he inscribed a book to commemorate his taking the habit.[39] One commendator, Ninian Fleming at Whithorn, voluntarily took the habit and was in trouble over it, as this was against the terms of his appointment.[40] Even resignation in favour or with retention was sometimes beneficial. Alexander Myln of Cambuskenneth made use of it.[41] The reforming abbot of Kinloss, Thomas Crystal, resigned in favour of Robert Reid, who continued the work of reform.[42] Reid in turn, and Walter Malin at Glenluce, used the system to train their successor as abbot and so avoid an unsuitable royal appointment.[43]

Under-age commendators always had a monastic administrator, usually some abbot, though at Paisley the prior held this office during the young John Hamilton's minority. Alexander Myln was administrator at Holyrood and St Andrews while James V's sons were minors; the abbots of Soulseat and Lindores also acted as administrators. Nor were the trends invariably in a less monastic direction. It was not unusual, in the period before Flodden, for an already professed monk to become abbot in succession to one who had only become a monk on being appointed abbot. Even in the later period, a regular abbot could succeed a commendator and quite often did so. To take just one monastery each of Black and White monks and Black and White canons, this happened at Kilwinning in 1527 when Alexander Hamilton succeeded Archbishop James Beaton; at Glenluce in 1519 when Walter Malin succeeded Bishop David Hamilton; at Dryburgh in 1523 when the same bishop was succeeded by James Stewart; and at Holyrood in 1528 James V's letter to Rome stated explicitly that Robert Cairncross (mentioned above) was a regular abbot succeeding a commendator.

By 1560 two thirds of Scottish monasteries had commendators; or conversely, one third did not.[44] In 1560 Rome was still providing regular abbots, for instance Thomas Hay at Glenluce, and was refusing to grant commends of monasteries not already held as such. Donald Campbell, abbot of Coupar Angus, was nominated bishop of Brechin but the pope in 1558 refused to let him retain the monastery as a commend, so the appointment was never effective.

The contrast with the Continent is striking. In Mediterranean lands commendation was all but universal and wreaked havoc as laymen moved into monasteries with their families and plundered everything, so that great abbeys were reduced to ruins and the monks were left destitute. In Scotland monks retained their individual portion (allowance) intact; they might have difficulty in getting it out of the commendator, but the law was on their side.[45] The bulls of appointment obliged Scottish commendators to use a quarter of the abbatial revenues for the upkeep of the buildings.[46]

Commendation in Scotland came late, developed slowly and was less stark and harmful than elsewhere. Dom David Knowles, so rightly and so highly esteemed as a monastic historian, unfortunately wrote that commendation could be seen at its worst in Scotland at the end of the fifteenth century, and Scottish historians have embroidered that judgement.[47] The reality is that Scotland had a late and mild form of commendation not found elsewhere, with never once a layman as commendator. It is also very probable that only Scotland experienced the half-way measure of non-monks taking the habit and making monastic vows on becoming abbot, for the monastic historians do not mention it happening elsewhere.

## NOTES

1. *Cambusk. Reg.*, no. 98; *Arbroath Lib.*, ii, pp. 208–10; R. K. Hannay, 'A Chapter Election at St. Andrews in 1417', *SHR* xiii (1916), pp. 321–7. For similar descriptions of episcopal elections see Dowden, *Medieval Church*, pp. 31–6; *St A. Form.*, i, pp. 332–4, 343–5.
2. This chapter relies much on Dilworth, 'Commendator System'. Other references are supplementary.
3. G. P. Innes, 'Ecclesiastical Patronage … in Scotland in the later middle ages', *RSCHS*, xiii (1957), pp. 73–83.
4. *Ibid.*, p. 79; *St A. Cop.*, pp. 89, 435.
5. *Vet. Mon.*, no. 597.
6. *St A. Cop.*, pp. liv–lv.
7. Schmitz, *Histoire*, iv, pp. 233–9.
8. Knowles, *Christian Monasticism*, p. 121 uses the term with its modern meaning, commendation being practically unknown in England.
9. Abundant evidence can be found in the various volumes of CPL, CSSR and ACSB.
10. Coulton, *Scottish Abbeys*, pp. 216–18.
11. *ADCP*, pp. xlv–xlix; *MRHS*, pp. 16–19; *Source Book*, ii, pp. 83–89.
12. Cartularies are listed in G. R. C. Davis, *Medieval Cartularies of Great Britain* (London, 1958) 129–37. Many collections of family charters are held in SRO. Gifts and Deposits (GD), and the SRO has its own 'house collection' of documents (RH 6). There are also collections by individuals and compilations by scholars, e.g. *Wigt. Chrs.*
13. Dilworth, 'Iona', pp. 80–1; Watt, *Fasti*, pp. 207–8. See also pp. 59–60 below.
14. There is no discrepancy with Dilworth, 'Commendator System', pp. 57, 62, 65, where these four monasteries are included in the figure of 39.
15. *Vet. Mon.*, nos 926–7.
16. Herkless & Hannay, *Archbishops*, ii, pp. 108, 116, 144–5.
17. *Vet. Mon.*, nos 922, 926; *Scots Peerage*, i, p. 22.
18. *ACSB*, pp. xxviii–xxxvii, xli.
19. Hannay, 'Papal Bulls', pp. 26–7; SRO, GD 124/9/14–21.
20. NLS, Acc. 7750, 1/22.
21. *RSS*, ii, no. 2366.
22. *St. A Form.*, i, pp. 304–5.
23. *ADCP*, pp. xlix–liii; *MRHS*, pp. 20–2; Source Book, ii, pp. 89–91; Cowan, 'Monastic Ideal', pp. 29–30.
24. Dilworth, *Whithorn*, p. 5; *Vet. Mon.*, no. 925; *Scots Peerage*, i, pp. 152–4.
25. *James V Letters*, pp. 3, 13, 72–3; *Wigt. Chrs*, pp. 42–6; *St A. Form.*, i, pp. 119–20.
26. *ADCP*, pp. 113, 130–1.
27. *St A. Form.*, i, pp. 39–40, 42–3, 55–6; *C. A. Chrs*, ii, pp. 275–7; *Scots Peerage*, i, pp. 336–7.
28. *St A. Form.*, i, pp. 336–9; *James V Letters*, p. 155; Brady, *Episcopal Succession*, i, p. 202.
29. Brady, *Episcopal Succession*, i, pp. 177–8; *CPL*, xiv, p. 43; Dilworth, 'Border Abbeys', pp. 240, 243.
30. *Dunfermline Reg.*, pp. 388–90, 397–8; Watt, *Fasti*, p. 308; *DSCHT*, p. 266.
31. Their careers are outlined in Dowden, *Bishops*.
32. *Crossraguel Chrs*, i, pp. 79, 91; *RSS*, ii, no. 642; *Scots Peerage*, ii, pp. 461–2.

33. *James V Letters*, pp. 235, 357–8, 426; Dunbar, *Scot. Kings*, pp. 238–9, excluding Adam Stewart, for whom see n. 35 below.
34. Brady, *Episcopal Succession*, i, pp. 166–7, 186–7; Hannay, 'Papal Bulls', pp. 25–7; Lees, *Paisley*, App. N.
35. Dilworth, 'Social Origins', pp. 203–4. See also p. 52 below.
36. Herkless & Hannay, *Archbishops*, ii, pp. 178, 235.
37. *Dunfermline Ct. Bk*, pp. 165, 192; Dilworth, 'Border Abbeys', pp. 241, 242–3; *St A. Form.*, i, pp. 181–2; ii, pp. 329–31; Finnie, 'House of Hamilton', p. 9; McRoberts, 'Culross', pp. 96–7. For a fuller list see p. 84 below.
38. Dilworth, 'Commendator System', n. 84–5, 96; Sanderson, *Mary Stewart's People*, pp. 166–9.
39. J. Durkan in *The Bibliotheck*, xi, no. 2 (1982), p. 35.
40. Dilworth, *Whithorn*, p. 7.
41. *St A. Form.*, ii, pp. 92–4.
42. Ferrerius, *Historia*, pp. 39–40, 84.
43. Ross, 'Religious Orders', pp. 213–14; *Kinloss Recs*, pp. 66–8; *St A. Form.*, ii, pp. 345–9.
44. For the evidence for each house and for regular abbots succeeding commendators, see Dilworth, 'Commendator System', pp. 62–5.
45. See p. 78 below.
46. For instance, *Wigt. Chrs*, nos 57, 78, 87; Hannay, 'Papal Bulls', p. 27; Lees, *Paisley*, App. N.
47. Knowles, *Christian Monasticism*, pp. 121, 144.

# 3

# *The Quality of Monastic Life*

Scotland in the sixteenth century did not provide a favourable ambience for a peaceful monastic life. The slaughter of so many churchmen at Flodden in 1513 led to strife between rival candidates for major church benefices. The death of James IV in battle brought about a royal minority, for James V was only seventeen months old when he succeeded, and in 1542 Mary Stewart became queen when just one week old. The resulting weakness of central government led to instability and lawlessness, a situation compounded by the English invasions.

Many monasteries lay in the path of the invading troops and thus suffered destruction of crops and buildings and even loss of life.[1] The Border abbeys suffered in 1523, and again and repeatedly in the 1540s. And not only the Border monasteries. Holyrood was despoiled, monks of Newbattle were taken prisoner to England, monasteries in the Firths of Forth and Tay were attacked. Inchcolm was occupied by troops, first English and then French; the monks left the island and did not return. There was other violence too, as for instance when Gordon of Lochinvar despoiled Glenluce in 1524[2] and a mob attacked Lindores in 1543.

There was strife and even violence at abbatial level too. The Crown was intervening increasingly, and when the Crown was weak all the other interests strove for power. Rival candidates sought abbacies. There was a long and complex struggle for Melrose from 1486 to 1510,[3] and the well-known incident in 1513 when the earl of Glencairn broke into Kilwinning and tried by physical force to make the abbot resign.[4]

Humes seized Coldingham, Kers took over Kelso; two priors of Coldingham were murdered.[5] At Kilwinning the abbot and the bailie were at loggerheads; at Glenluce Kennedys and Gordons, rivals to be bailie, disputed with each other and with the abbot.[6]

Nevertheless, despite the state of the country and the strife between rival abbatial candidates, corporate morale in the monasteries seems to have remained high. In five of the six disputes between 1516 and 1529 mentioned in the last chapter, the community elected one of themselves to be abbot in spite of the pressures on them not to do so. Trail was a dependent priory, without a community but still belonging to Holyrood. In 1528 the Holyrood canons presented one of their own community to the bishop of Galloway as prior of Trail, for which they were rebuked by the Privy Council. Nevertheless they did exactly the same again in 1558.[7]

At Melrose in 1556–7 the community confronted the commendator several times over his neglect of the buildings and the fall in the number of monks. Despite his furious reaction they stood their ground and succeeded in having the number raised to sixteen.[8] An abbot of Melrose appeared at the general chapter at Cîteaux in 1562, a time when the abbey lacked an effectively appointed superior and the Crown was administering its finances;[9] he would seem to have been a Melrose monk elected by his brethren. Choir office was continued in some monasteries after 1560 and the Dunfermline community in particular retained corporate solidarity.[10]

Two things in monasteries invariably decline when efforts are not made to maintain them – the intake of recruits and the state of the buildings – and efforts are not made unless a future is envisaged. Recruitment of young monks continued right up to 1560, as will be seen in the next chapter, while buildings were maintained and in some places new ones were erected. Recruitment and upkeep of buildings are both signs of corporate morale.

In speaking of the state of monastic buildings in the sixteenth century a difficulty has to be faced. The documents of the period habitually overstate, describing buildings as totally ruined or almost level with the ground, and then one finds monks living in them, or perhaps the church in use, as in fact happened at Jedburgh in 1550.[11] Reports of buildings in ruins are therefore to be treated with caution unless verified from another source. There is, however, one unusually factual and nuanced report given to the consistory of cardinals at Rome in 1517, in which one tower of Kelso church is said to contain tuneful bells while the other is old and weak. Perhaps the accuracy is due to its being testimony given under oath.[12]

Abbots Thomas Crystal and Robert Reid of Kinloss repaired and rebuilt the church and monastic buildings at both Kinloss and Beauly and carried out repair work in appropriated parish churches.[13] There was repair work and rebuilding at Cambuskenneth under Alexander Myln, also at Paisley.[14] Much of the west range and the precinct wall at St Andrews date from the sixteenth century, and indeed St Andrews provides one of the greatest signs of vitality and confidence in the future, namely the opening of St Leonard's College in 1512, whatever adaptation the buildings may have needed.[15] New buildings were erected at half a dozen other monasteries, though perhaps not on a very large scale.[16] There is also evidence of repair work in the 1540s and 1550s, including that at Paisley after a fire, at Jedburgh after the invasions and at Melrose when the monks confronting the commendator in 1556–7 insisted on the church being repaired.[17] It adds up to much activity and employment and considerable benefit to the economy, even if one cannot discount the references to neglected buildings.[18]

This building activity is evidence of vitality and of confidence in the future. The furnishing within the monasteries leads to the same conclusion. The Renaissance scholar Ferrerio recounts in detail the notable acquisitions for the church and sacristy at Kinloss. In 1520, for instance, a monk was sent to Flanders to buy vestments and other equipment, and in 1538 a painter was brought in to make paintings in the chapels.[19] In some ways Kinloss under its two reforming abbots was a special case but an abbot of Fearn, who died in 1485, bought an organ as well as furnishings and *pulchra ornamenta* (beautiful adornments) from Flanders.[20] The description of Kelso and Arbroath in 1517 included organs, bells, furnishings and Mass gear, giving a picture of a certain magnificence with no hint of decline or defeatism.[21]

There was at this period a tendency for the abbot's quarters to become a separate house and for the monks to be given more privacy. Partitions were installed in the dorter at Crossraguel and perhaps elsewhere, and little houses in the garden at Pittenweem. The little houses in the garden at Crossraguel could have been for pensioners, monks or seculars.[22] To put this into perspective, it should be mentioned that a large measure of privacy is nowadays taken for granted in Benedictine monasteries.

In most, perhaps all, Scottish monasteries in the sixteenth century (except of course in the Perth charterhouse) each monk or canon had his own portion, that is his personal allowance, usually a generous one.[23] It consisted of such items as grain for bread and brewing ale, money to buy meat and fish, 'habit siller' (clothes allowance) and perhaps pittances (small bonuses).[24] The firm impression is given that it was really a salary, for the monk had a right to it. There are cases of monks before 1560 taking successful legal action if their portion was not paid, and also of a monk's portion before 1560 being given to an outsider.[25]

Some monastic officials, for instance the prior at Melrose and Scone, had a double portion; some monks too had servants, though we do not know how many.[26] Often monks had their particular yaird (vegetable garden) and one is recorded as selling kail from his.[27] At Kinloss there are references to silver vessels and the like gifted to the church by individual monks,[28] and it is difficult to see how they could do this unless by accumulated savings from their portions. It certainly seems that monks in effect had property and an income and were well looked after, a situation which was not scandalous in itself but was a watering down of communal monastic life. Not that common life was altogether lacking. At Kelso, although the abbot's dwelling was separate from that of the monks, they shared a common table, and at Cambuskenneth under Alexander Myln clothing was given out from a common stock and a canon read aloud at the community meals.[29]

The chief task of monks and regular canons in monasteries is the communal choir office, and every indication is that this continued without interruption unless war prevented it. There are very few references to it; it was taken for granted. At Kelso there were two daily sung Masses, one for the founder and one according to the calendar, while at Arbroath there were two daily sung Masses and often three.[30] Sixteenth-century missals from Cambuskenneth and Paisley have survived, and a breviary from Arbroath.[31] Matins at Arbroath, a large Benedictine abbey, was at midnight[32] (which is stricter than St Benedict's Rule).

At a visitation at Pittenweem in 1554, the canons were instructed to ring the bell for matins at the sixth hour in summer and the seventh in winter,[33] which in our time would be respectively midnight and roughly 1.30 a.m. It could hardly have been at 6 and 7 o'clock (our time), given that townspeople's work usually began at 5 and Mass was at 5 in summer and 6 in winter.[34]

It is not a simple matter to reconstruct a monastic horarium. For one thing, day and night were each divided into twelve hours; and for another, the further north one went, the more the length of the hour varied between summer and winter. Even in south Italy, where Benedict wrote his Rule, the day varied a fair amount according to the season. One can, however, safely say that matins usually began well before dawn, between 2 and 3.30 (modern time), while Carthusian matins lasted from before midnight until about 2 a.m.[35] This daily round of choir office continued in every monastery with a community up to the disturbances of 1559–60 and even after.

An attempt should be made to assess the moral state of the monasteries, despite one obvious difficulty. Just as news items are not about people not involved in accidents or not appearing in court, so there is no record of monks quietly performing their monastic duties; it is always infringements that are recorded. One area likely to be chronicled is sexual lapses. Ferrerio tells of three unchaste abbots of Kinloss in the fifteenth century and two at its daughter-house, Culross. Of an abbot who died in 1504 he writes that the man was quite pious but for indulging in pleasures of the flesh and unchastity.[36] Ferrerio was self-consciously a renaissance man and no doubt wanting to show he was broad-minded, but this is rather like saying that a senior policeman was quite good at his job except for a little heroin trafficking.

The record of abbots and commendators in this regard was not good, to judge from the legitimations of their offspring,[37] but only two ordinary monks or regular canons had their children legitimated in the period 1500–1560: a canon of Holyrood, vicar of St Cuthbert's, in 1508 and a monk of Balmerino in 1553.[38] Only the sons were usually legitimated, and only to give them rights over property, so illegitimate children would always have been much more numerous than legitimations; but two cases in sixty years is not a very black record. When Sir David Lindsay wrote in his *Ane Satyre of the Thrie Estaitis*:

> Speir at the monkis of Balmirrynoch
> Gife lichery be syn,[39]

he may well have had in mind not the ordinary Balmerino monks but the abbot Robert Forester, a Cistercian monk before becoming abbot, who had three sons and a daughter legitimated.[40]

There were of course incidents such as would feature in news items nowadays. A monk of Kinloss in 1500 committed manslaughter through beating a boy in the cloister, went to Rome for absolution but never returned.[41] Patrick Yester in 1559 committed manslaughter at Balmerino, but claimed it was accidental and later received Crown remission.[42] A monk of Coupar Angus received papal absolution for sacrilege and theft. One should perhaps reserve judgment on the action taken by the abbot of Newbattle against the monks who refused to sing choir office because he would not increase their portions, for we have only his side of the story. We would like to know more about the prior and canons of Pittenweem being accused of murder and assault in the lands of Pittenweem in 1532.[43] The prior of Monymusk in 1534 took disciplinary action against a canon, more or less confining him to barracks, and strife was caused and office in choir suspended when the other canons took the delinquent's side.[44]

There is evidence on the credit side too. Ferrerio speaks of pious deathbeds at Kinloss.[45] Six Perth Carthusians achieved the distinction of *laudabiliter vixit*, the highest honour in the order and only conferred after careful investigation. According to a Carthusian historian, it is a 'record practically without parallel', yet it was achieved by the single Scottish charterhouse in the sixteenth century.[46] There is need for caution in assessing the moral and spiritual climate from isolated incidents, for there is not enough evidence to justify generalisations.

There is a monastic adage that a good monastery is not one where no faults are committed but one where faults do not go uncorrected. If we speak of moral shortcomings, we must also consider the two arrangements for maintaining monastic discipline: the general chapters, where the abbots of each group would meet at regular intervals, and the visitations carried out by someone with the authority to correct abuses. Originally Cistercian, both had been accepted by all the centralised groups and in 1215 the fourth Lateran Council imposed them on all uncentralised Benedictines and Augustinians. Later, bishops were expected to make visitations in their diocese, except in monasteries which had the privilege of exemption from episcopal authority.[47]

There is some evidence of Benedictine chapters held in Scotland in the thirteen and fourteenth centuries,[48] but by the fifteenth they were being held irregularly, if at all. In 1415 Pope Benedict XIII commissioned the abbot of Arbroath to summon a chapter of Benedictine abbots, as he had been told that reform was needed.[49] Then James I in 1425, the year after his return to Scotland, ordered Benedictines and Augustinians to hold chapters and reform themselves; in this he was following the example of Henry V of England, who had done precisely that with English Benedictines four years earlier.[50] There is no evidence of Benedictine or Augustinian chapters being held in Scotland after 1425. Certainly they were not held regularly, and if there was no general chapter there was no one appointed by the chapter to carry out visitations. As for Kelso and the other monasteries originating from Tiron, the series of reforming chapters initiated by Tiron in the late fifteenth century clearly did not affect Scotland.[51]

The two Cluniac abbeys, Paisley and Crossraguel, had the privilege of exemption from the bishop's jurisdiction. So did the Perth charterhouse and the White Monks and Canons, the Cistercians and Premonstratensians. The Valliscaulians were not exempt but thought they were. Augustinian canons on the whole were not exempt, though Holyrood had the privilege, at least for a time.[52] As for Benedictines, including the ex-Tironensians, one must look at each house singly. Iona, Kelso and Lindores apparently had the privilege, while the great abbey of Arbroath did not and was subject to visitations by the bishop.[53] The above is a rough summary and shows the complex state of affairs, compounded by archbishops of St Andrews sometimes being granted powers of a legate *a latere*, which included authority to conduct visitations of exempt monasteries.

The situation was further complicated if the monastic superior was a commendator hardly likely to welcome a visitation from outside. Nor were Scottish bishops in the sixteenth century, with responsibility for the non-exempt monasteries in the diocese, the ideal persons for reforming the lives of others. Exempt 'uncentralised' monasteries should have had visitations by someone endowed with special papal authority (or the powers of a legate *a latere*) but there is no evidence that this happened. Exempt monasteries in the centralised groups, on the other hand, should have undergone the visitations customary in their order. The Scottish reforming councils of 1549 and 1559 tried to address the problem, but by then it was too late.[54]

We can, however, see the efforts to reform discipline made within the centralised groups. The prior of Perth charterhouse was bound to attend the chapter at the Grande Chartreuse every leap year, and no doubt regular visitations of the house were made by some foreign prior.[55] Discipline was maintained; in fact an unsatisfactory prior was simply deposed. James V protested to the prior of the Grande Chartreuse in 1535 about the deposition of Prior Hugh.[56] As we shall see, royal intervention was a recurring feature; the Crown wanted reform of monastic life in theory but hindered it in practice.

In 1506 the prior of Val des Choux asked the prior of Beauly to carry out a visitation at Ardchattan. Very soon afterwards, the bishop of Ross wanted to conduct a visitation at Beauly, whereupon the prior wrote to Val des Choux asking for documents showing that Valliscaulians were exempt from episcopal authority. In December 1506, no doubt to his great surprise, the prior of Val des Choux replied that their houses were not exempt and in fact those in France received visitations from the local bishop. This was followed by a comprehensive rebuke: the Beauly prior had never gone to Val des Choux, nor had his predecessor, and he was therefore summoned to attend next year's general chapter. Attendance was obligatory every four or at least every six years. Nor had he ever sent '*pisces Salmones nuncupatos*' (fish called salmon) promised by his predecessor.[57]

The salmon was most likely a tribute due to a superior rather than an exotic gift. Probably that prior of Beauly neither sent a salmon nor attended a general chapter, and the subsequent history of the priory is obscure. Although said to have been transferred to the Cistercian order in 1510, its situation remained somewhat anomalous and eventually it was subjected to the abbot of Cistercian Kinloss.[58] As Pluscarden had already become Benedictine, only the small priory at Ardchattan remained as a clearly Valliscaulian house.

Premonstratensians were organised in regional groups called circaries or circuits, with one abbot chosen by general chapter to conduct visitations within the group. By 1498 the Scottish houses were *de jure* and *de facto* in a circuit of their own, though quite possibly no Scottish abbot had attended general chapter or paid the customary dues for some time. At a reforming general chapter at Prémontré in 1505, to which all abbots were summoned, the abbot of Soulseat was appointed visitor in Scotland; he was the only Scot who attended. About the same time, however, James IV wrote asking for the prior of Whithorn to be made visitor, and in 1507 wrote again asking for the abbot of Dryburgh to be appointed. The archbishop of St Andrews also wrote complaining of the Whithorn prior acting in his metropolitan province.

There was no clear primacy among the Scottish houses. Dryburgh, the first founded and reckoned the wealthiest, took precedence in the royal council, but Whithorn was a cathedral priory and the only house of White Canons with a mitred superior, while Soulseat was reckoned a daughter of Prémontré itself. In 1512 the English houses severed their connection with Prémontré;[59] the Scots, supposedly after some hesitation, remained within the order. Surprisingly, given the situation at Whithorn after 1516, its prior is said to have been the visitor for Scotland until 1523.

In 1523 John Maxwell, abbot of Holywood, was made visitor, but a few months later in December he was transferred to Dundrennan and became a Cistercian abbot. The abbot of Dryburgh, who succeeded him, was hardly the man to reform others. A second short-lived appointment was made in 1532 when the abbot of Soulseat became visitor, only to die that same year. Although the prior of Whithorn then succeeded, Scotland is mentioned for the last time in the acts of general chapter in 1534. The Scottish Crown's nomination of commendators and unsuitable superiors had thwarted all efforts to reform.[60]

In the later middle ages Cluny's influence declined, but towards the end of the fifteenth century its general chapter embarked on sustained reforming activity.[61] The Cluniac dependent priories in England had been in great difficulties during the Great Schism; they never really recovered, and in 1480 all were exempted from Cluny's authority.[62] Paisley and Crossraguel, however, retained their relations with Cluny, although as abbeys they enjoyed a good measure of autonomy. In addition the privilege of exemption from episcopal authority still held good for all Cluniac houses. Successive archbishops of Glasgow recognised this, and in 1516 Andrew Forman, archbishop of St Andrews, declared that though as legate *a latere* he had powers of visitation in exempt monasteries, he would not use these for Paisley and Crossraguel.[63] There is evidence of their continuing connection with Cluny and visitations may have been made, though no record of any has survived.[64]

Relations between Scotland and Cîteaux continued throughout the fifteenth century, even though attendance at general chapter was patchy.[65] The Cistercian system of filiation, whereby the abbot of a founding monastery had powers of supervision and visitation in the daughter-houses, had also continued to operate.[66] At the end of the century, general chapter took part in the widespread monastic reform in France, and we know of envoys from Cîteaux sent to Scotland. One was Thomas Fassington, a Scot and a monk of Cîteaux, whose commission in 1506 included visitation of the Scottish abbeys.[67] In 1517, when in Scotland again, he clashed with Andrew Forman, who claimed the right of visitation in the Cistercian houses in his diocese and forbade their abbots to receive Fassington.[68]

Nevertheless relations with Cîteaux never ceased and visitations seem to have taken place, conducted either by a Scots abbot commissioned by Cîteaux or by the abbot of the mother-house. Thomas Crystal of Kinloss, for instance, carried out visitations at the two daughter-houses, Culross and Deer, and when Kinloss and Deer disputed over teinds, the other abbots met and adjudicated in the matter.[69] One gets the impression of cohesion among Scottish Cistercians. We also have detailed accounts of one series of visitations in the 1530s, to be described below.

The general monastic reform in France towards the end of the fifteenth century affected even the uncentralised Augustinians, and one local reform was to influence two Scottish monasteries. A reform movement initiated at Windesheim in the Netherlands coalesced with John Standónck's efforts at reform for clerical university students, the aim being to produce priests dedicated to study and austere poverty. When St Andrews priory founded St Leonard's as a university college in 1512, its first principal was the Augustinian John Annand, who had known Standonck. The college was within the priory precinct and was run on monastic lines, with a very strict regime for all students, whether they were Augustinians or not. It was later to have great significance for the Scottish Reformation.[70]

In 1518 Alexander Myln was provided as abbot of Cambuskenneth. Though not a canon previously, he took his monastic duties seriously and sent some of his young canons to the celebrated Augustinian monastery of St Victor in Paris, which had been influenced by Windesheim and Standonck. His aim was to raise the academic level and introduce strict monastic observance. Cambuskenneth, incidentally, had been founded from Arrouaise in northern France, the centre of a strict group of monasteries, but probably had had no relations with the mother-house for a very long time. In fact the last general chapter at Arrouaise was in 1470.[71]

Robert Richardson (he latinised his name as Richardinus), who later became a Protestant clergyman in England, was one of those sent to Paris, where he published a commentary on the Rule of St Augustine, dedicated to Myln.[72] In it he described lax observance, as well as laying down what should be done about it. Unfortunately the book is rendered almost worthless by general moralising, extravagant denunciation and unintelligent formalism. In fact it tells us hardly anything, for it is seldom clear if Richardson is speaking about Scotland or France. The flavour of the book can be judged from a lengthy and not untypical passage on the evils inflicted by women on the human race, for one of the instances adduced to prove his point is that John the Baptist survived living with dragons and scorpions in the desert but met his death when he tangled with Herodias.[73] Myln did, however, raise the academic and monastic level at Cambuskenneth, and it is worth noting that these often went together.[74]

At the turn of the century Thomas Crystal, a monk of Kinloss, was made abbot at the age of thirty. For the next thirty years he was an almost ideal abbot, energetic and dedicated, improving every facet of the monastery and increasing the number of monks. In 1528, wishing the good work to continue, he resigned in favour of a secular priest, Robert Reid, who was an office-bearer in Moray diocese. Reid duly took the habit and was blessed as a regular abbot. He went in person to Rome to collect his bulls of provision and in Paris on his way back was introduced by Robert Richardson to Giovanni Ferrerio from Piedmont, a typical Renaissance scholar. Ferrerio travelled to Scotland with Reid and eventually settled at Kinloss to teach the young monks.

It is Ferrerio's various accounts that tell us what we know of Kinloss at this period. Naturally he was prejudiced in favour of Reid and his predecessor Crystal, but the hard facts make it clear that Kinloss was in a healthy and flourishing condition. In 1531 Reid, though he continued as abbot of Kinloss, was made commendator of Beauly, where he restored the buildings, put in officials from Kinloss, received novices and brought them to Kinloss to study under Ferrerio.[75] As at St Andrews and Cambuskenneth, study and reformed monastic observance went together.

Two visitations of Scottish monasteries are well documented, but before they are dealt with some explanation is needed. Acts of visitation (that is, the enactments made by the investigator) have been called the pathology of monastic life, not revealing the general health but only particular illnesses. From the monastic point of view it is bad news if monks spend the day in taverns or carouse after Compline, but good news if the authorities do not allow it to continue. One cannot generalise from the visitation of a particular monastery; possibly conditions were better elsewhere and such abuses did not occur, or possibly they were worse because such abuses were allowed to continue.

At Pittenweem, a dependent priory of St Andrews, a fairly thorough visitation was carried out in 1554 by John Winram, subprior of St Andrews and later a superintendent in the Reformed Church.[76] Its provisions are well known,[77] and what is significant is not the run-of-the-mill relaxed discipline which they show but rather the fact that the monastic authorities of St Andrews were not prepared to let them continue.

The Cistercian visitations of the 1530s resemble a stubbornly waged campaign. In 1530 the general chapter at Cîteaux made Walter Malin, abbot of Glenluce, the visitor for Scotland. James V, however, found him too zealous and in January 1531 wrote to Cîteaux asking for a special abbot visitor. The abbot of Chaalis was appointed, came to Scotland and acted with firmness and some severity, laying down strict regulations and disciplining some monks. James then asked Cîteaux to restore the status quo. The general chapter of 1533, however, supported the visitor. The abbot of Melrose, Andrew Durie, had been summoned to the same chapter to answer for his negligence, but James intervened to prevent his going.

The chapter of 1533 appointed two Scots abbots as visitors for five years, Walter Malin of Glenluce and Donald Campbell of Coupar Angus; they likewise supported what the French visitor had done. Their main thrust was to restore strict common life, with no private portions or gardens or 'habit siller'; instead all necessities were to be supplied by monastic officials from a common stock. To cut a long story short, monks of Melrose and its daughter-houses Newbattle and Balmerino protested and argued, and the general chapter of 1535 allowed the two Scots abbots to modify the French abbot's regulations. The outcome was that portions remained but the worst abuses against the common life were removed; for instance, a monk was no longer to keep what remained unused of his portion. It was a not unreasonable compromise.[78]

The surviving documentation of this episode is considerable; and not only that, but it includes some disciplinary enactments of the visitors, which have scarcity value. The involvement of James V, shown by the royal correspondence, enhances the sensational aspect. Scottish historians have therefore, very understandably perhaps, tended to treat the whole episode in isolation, whereas it should rather be seen in the context of continuing efforts towards reform on the part of general chapters in France and a number of monastic superiors in Scotland. Later we find a monk of Kinloss arguing in favour of strict common life, and in 1553 the abbot and monks of Coupar Angus agreed to institute this.[79] Walter Malin was still abbot-visitor in 1556 and that same year the archbishop of St Andrews protested at the disciplinary action taken by him against six monks at Newbattle.[80]

To sum up, the evidence is fragmentary and the standard of observance seems to have varied considerably between monasteries, but in some houses at least there were genuine and sustained efforts towards reform. And if there was little indication of real fervour, there was also very little that was downright scandalous. It certainly seems that Scottish monastic life in the sixteenth century would have been better but for the interference of the Scottish Crown and, to a lesser extent, the opposition of the archbishops of St Andrews. If a sudden end to monastic life had not come in 1560, Scotland might well have moved in the direction of reforms on the Continent by allowing abbots to be controlled by the Crown while the prior and monks led their monastic life regardless of who enjoyed the abbatial revenues.[81]

## NOTES

1. MRHS, p. 27 and passim. References to this source will not be repeated. Ross, 'Religious Orders', pp. 212–13; McRoberts, 'Material Destruction', pp. 420–5.
2. *Wigt. Chrs*, pp. 46–8, 62–5.
3. Dilworth, 'Border Abbeys', pp. 242–3. Cowan, 'Monastic Ideal', pp. 30–4 summarises a number of these disputes over monasteries.
4. *Liber Protocollorum M. Cuthberti Simonis* (Grampian Club, 1875), i, pp. 544–50; ii, pp. 477–81; 'Kilwinning Collections', pp. 180–3.
5. Dilworth, 'Border Abbeys', pp. 120–2; Morton, *Monastic Annals*, p. 96.
6. Henry, 'Glenluce', pp. 139–47, 157–76. For bailies see pp. 46–8 below.
7. R. C. Reid, 'The Priory of St Mary's Isle', TDGAS, 3rd Ser. 36 (1957–8), pp. 13–25; ADCP, p. 288.
8. *Melrose Recs*, iii, pp. 150–1, 155–61, 217–19; Ross, 'Religious Orders', pp. 219–20.
9. Canivez, *Statuta*, 1562, no. 47; Dilworth, 'Monks and Ministers', pp. 202–3.
10. *Ibid.*, p. 216; Cowan, 'Monastic Ideal', p. 43.
11. Dilworth, 'Border Abbeys', p. 236; McRoberts, 'Material Destruction', pp. 423, 425.
12. *Vet. Mon.*, no. 927.
13. Ferrerius, *Historia*, pp. 26, 28, 41, 47, 70–3.
14. *Cambusk. Reg.*, pp. 122, 296; Durkan, 'Paisley', pp. 111–13, 124.
15. Dilworth, 'Canons', pp. 164–6.
16. I have been greatly helped by reading the chapter on the monasteries in Dr Richard Fawcett's forthcoming book on Scottish architecture. He is of course not responsible for any inaccuracies or change of emphasis which I may have introduced.
17. McRoberts, 'Material Destruction', pp. 425–7, 437–8, 441; Durkan, 'Paisley', p. 120.
18. For instance, *James V Letters*, pp. 420–1; McRoberts, 'Material Destruction', pp. 425–6.
19. Ferrerius, *Historia*, passim, especially pp. 50–1, 75.
20. Backmund, *Monasticon*, ii, pp. 104–5.
21. *Vet. Mon.*, nos 926–7.
22. Cowan, 'Ayrshire Abbeys', p. 278; Ross, 'Religious Orders', p. 225. Cf. Knowles, *Christian Monasticism*, p. 103.
23. Sanderson, *Mary Stewart's People*, pp. 107–8.
24. ADCP, p. lvi; *Wigt. Chrs*, p. 56; *Melrose Recs*, iii, pp. 139, 146; *St A. Form.*, ii, pp. 189–90; SRO, CH 8/18, fos 2–6.
25. For examples see pp. 48, 78 below.
26. RSS, viii, no. 1374; *Scone Lib.*, p. 216.
27. Ferrerius, *Historia*, pp. 52–3.
28. *Ibid.*, pp. 29, 33.
29. *Vet. Mon.*, no. 927; Richardinus, *Commentary*, pp. 92, 127.
30. *Vet. Mon.*, nos 926–7. Cf. Schmitz, *Histoire*, vi, p. 167.
31. W. J. Anderson, 'Three sixteenth-century Scottish Missals', IR ix (1958), pp. 204–7; J. B. L. Tolhurst, 'Notes on a printed Monastic Breviary used at Arbroath Abbey', IR v (1954), pp. 104–18.
32. *Vet. Mon.*, no. 926.
33. NLS, Adv. 29.4.2 (vi), fo. 107v; Ross, 'Religious Orders', p. 225.
34. McRoberts, Essays, pp. 85, 104.

35. Schmitz, *Histoire*, vi, pp. 166–7; Knowles, *Religious Orders*, ii, pp. 238–9.
36. Ferrerius, *Historia*, pp. 28–35.
37. Listed in Fleming, *Reformation*, pp. 540–69. The three canons listed on pp. 546, 562, 568 were secular cathedral canons. See also Dilworth, 'Commendator System', pp. 61–2, 66.
38. *RSS*, i, no. 1610; iv, no. 2117.
39. *The Works of Sir David Lindsay*, ed. D. Hamer, ii (STS 1931), p. 50.
40. Fleming, *Reformation*, pp. 549, 555–6, 562; RSS, ii, no. 2157; iii, nos 2399, 2554; iv, no. 2431; *MRHS*, p. 73.
41. Ferrerius, *Historia*, p. 33.
42. *Melrose Recs*, iii, pp. 163–4; *RSS*, v, no. 2362.
43. *St A. Form.*, i, pp. 274–5, 308–9; ii, pp. 4–9.
44. *A. B. Ill.*, iii, pp. 488–9, 490–6; Dilworth, 'Dependent Priories', p. 63.
45. Ferrerius, *Historia*, pp. 33, 38.
46. Hogg, 'Perth Charterhouse', p. 168; Beckett, 'Perth Charterhouse', p. 63.
47. Schmitz, *Histoire*, iii, pp. 48–50; Dickinson, *Origins*, p. 82.
48. *CPL*, i, p. 231; ii, p. 545; *Arbroath Lib.*, i, p. 314; G. F. Duckett, *Charters and Records of the Ancient Abbey of Cluni 1077–1534* (1888), ii, p. 121.
49. *St. A. Cop.*, p. 444.
50. *Source Book*, ii, pp. 98–9; Knowles, *Religious Orders*, ii, pp. 182–3.
51. Schmitz, *Histoire*, iii, pp. 205–9.
52. Dickinson, *Origins*, p. 79, 162; *Vet. Mon.*, no. 855; *James V Letters*, p. 203.
53. CPL i, p. 504; vii, pp. 170, 455; *Kelso Lib.*, nos 529, 532; *Vet. Mon.*, nos 335, 927.
54. Winning, 'Church Councils', pp. 338–9, 351; Patrick, *Statutes*, pp. 94–5, 167–8.
55. Thompson, *Carthusian Order*, p. 248; Beckett, 'Perth Charterhouse', pp. 51–66.
56. *James V Letters*, p. 300.
57. *Beauly Chrs*, pp. 140–2, 157–62; NLS, MS 2101, fos 260v, 267v–269v; Dilworth, 'Franco-Scottish Efforts'.
58. *James V Letters*, pp. 194–5, 345–6; Ferrerius, *Historia*, p. 40.
59. Knowles, *Religious Orders*, ii, pp. 142–3; Talbot, *Letters*, p. 251.
60. Dilworth, *Whithorn*, pp. 7–8; 'Franco-Scottish Efforts'. The period 1498–1534 is covered by Backmund, *Monasticon*, ii, pp. 92–6, 100; 'Order in Scotland', 28–32. His account in places is difficult to reconcile with Scottish sources.
61. Schmitz, *Histoire*, iii, pp. 205–7, 213; A. Renaudet in *French Humanism 1470–1600*, ed. W. L. Gundersheimer (London, 1969), pp. 67, 77–8.
62. Knowles, *Religious Orders*, ii, pp. 158–61.
63. *Crossraguel Chrs*, i, pp. 43–5, 46–8, 64–7.
64. *Ibid.*, i, p. 68; Fergusson, 'Last Monks', pp. 56–7, 61; Dilworth, 'Franco-Scottish Efforts'.
65. Canivez, *Satuta*, passim; Morton, *Monastic Annals*, p. 238.
66. Ferrerius, *Historia*, pp. 29, 31, 62; *CPL*, vii, pp. 214, 346–7.
67. Talbot, *Letters*, pp. 109–10, 231–2; *RSS*, i, nos 1363, 2833; *James IV Letters*, p. 29; Ross, 'Religious Orders', p. 214.
68. Talbot, *Letters*, pp. 233–4, 245–7; *St. A. Form*, i, p. 56.
69. Canivez, *Statuta*, p. 1510, no. 46; p. 1518, no. 35; Ferrerius, *Historia*, pp. 69, 79–80; *C. A. Chrs*, ii, p. 275; Dilworth, 'Franco-Scottish Efforts'.
70. Herkless & Hannay, *St Leonard*; *St A. Acta*, pp. xliii–1; Ross, 'Religious Orders', pp. 193, 195; Dilworth, 'Canons', pp. 165–6, 171–2. Renaudet, pp. 67, 74–6, 79–80.

71. DHGE, iv, pp. 728–30.
72. Durkan, 'Evangelicals', pp. 134–7, 148–9.
73. Richardinus, *Commentary*, p. 112.
74. Dilworth, 'Canons', pp. 166–9.
75. Ferrerius, *Historia*, passim, especially pp. 35–6, 39–40.
76. DSCHT, p. 876.
77. NLS, Adv. 29.4.2 (vi), fo. 107v; Ross, 'Religious Orders', p. 225.
78. Canivez, *Statuta*, pp. 1530–1, 1533, 1535; *James V Letters*, pp. 177, 187, 202, 210–11, 238, 286–7; ADCP, pp. 347–8, 360; *Wigt. Chrs*, no. 46. The visitors' degrees are in *A. B. Ill.*, iv, pp. 5–18, with translation in *Transactions of the Aberdeen Ecclesiological Society*, x (1897), pp. 171–9. There is much in secondary works, e.g. Morton, *Monastic Annals*, pp. 240–2; Ross, 'Religious Orders', pp. 217–18. The episode is dealt with more fully in Dilworth, 'Franco-Scottish Efforts'.
79. Ross, 'Religious Orders' 215; *C. A. Chrs*, ii, 109–10.
80. *Wigt. Chrs*, p. 65n; *Melrose Recs*, pp. 150, 188, 192.
81. Dilworth, 'Commendator System', p. 53.

# 4

# *Economics and Personnel*

Beyond any doubt most Scottish monasteries were wealthy, some very wealthy indeed. In 1560, when the pound Scots was worth one fifth of sterling, the annual income of St Andrews was £12,500, at Arbroath £11,000, at Dunfermline £9,600. There was then a big drop to Paisley with £6,000. Scone, Holyrood and Coupar Angus had £5,500. Melrose, Lindores and Kelso were around the £5,000 mark. Pluscarden, Kinloss and Cambuskenneth had £3,000–£4,000. At £2,000–£3,000 come Coldingham, Kilwinning, Deer, Jedburgh, Dryburgh and Whithorn; their income was one fifth of St Andrews, and a quarter of Arbroath and Dunfermline. No doubt the assets of the Border abbeys had been eroded by invasion and destruction. Monasteries with a by no means negligible community had between £1,500 and £2,000; such were Crossraguel, Balmerino, Culross, Newbattle, the Perth charterhouse, Inchmahome. Another dozen had an income below £1,000 yearly.[1] To give an idea of the wealth, £20 a year was considered enough for a priest to live on, while some curates had just two thirds of this, 20 marks.[2]

There were, however, financial disadvantages. It was an era of steady inflation in Scotland, and monasteries were taxed heavily by the Crown. Purchasing the bulls at Rome for the provision of an abbot was very expensive; not only that, but considerable pensions were being paid out of monastic income. A large fraction of the revenues went to the abbot personally, perhaps not earmarked for him but disposed of by him. If the abbot was a commendator or a royal official, this was really a form of taxation. Buildings needed upkeep or major repairs, a liability compounded by the damage done by war and invasion not only to the buildings but also to the land which was the primary source of monastic income, though some monasteries had other sources of revenue, such as the wool trade or coal-mining.[3] In general terms, the monasteries had considerable wealth but also heavy liabilities.

It was of course a land or farming economy. Land was rented out, even by the Cistercians, who in early times had farmed it themselves, for the era of laybrothers doing the farm work was long since over. There is a well-known passage in John Major's *Historia Maioris Britanniae*, published in 1521, of which an English translation is easily available. The translation is unfortunately seriously misleading, for it speaks of unworthy monastic superiors who may have lined their own pockets and 'brought ruin on the farmer-tenants of the convent by raising their rents'. Major, however, did not say that farmer-tenants were ruined by having their rent raised but that oppressed (*pessundati*) workers on the land (*agricolae*) had the yield (*proventus*) due from them increased.[4] A very vague passage has been translated in specific and much stronger terms. In fact rents were not raised *pro rata* with inflation, which was one reason why monasteries lacked ready money.[5]

In many cases, in addition to the rent, the monastery received the teinds (10 per cent of the produce) as spiritual income. Often the monastery did not want the teinds paid in kind, in which case it could increase the rent to include their value or (what was much the same) sell the produce back for cash. The easiest solution was to lease all teinds for cash to a middle-man, who would then collect them for himself.[6] The Scottish church council of 1559 decreed that teinds were not to be leased, for the principal beneficiary was usually a layman whose aim was to get what he could.[7]

Appropriated parishes provided many monasteries with considerable income. Appropriation can be defined as the transfer of the revenues of a parish to a corporation, and of course the revenues came from the land endowment and tithes. In Europe, only Switzerland had a higher proportion of such transfers than Scotland, where by 1560 there were 890, 86% of the total number of parishes in the country.[8]

Monasteries were important beneficiaries of the system. Kelso and its dependent priory of Lesmahagow held the revenues of over 40 parishes. Arbroath had about 40; Holyrood with its priory of Trail, Paisley and St Andrews had about 30 each. Dunfermline, Cambuskenneth and Jedburgh with its priories each had about 20. Lindores had 17, Kilwinning had 16 (14 of them in Ayrshire), Whithorn had 14 (12 of them in Wigtownshire). Dryburgh had over a dozen and even little Ardchattan in the West Highlands had about half a dozen.[9]

These parishes had been founded with a church and revenues to provide for support of a priest, perhaps even two, upkeep of the fabric, the necessary gear, relief of the poor and so on. Then the lay founder or patron, wishing to shed responsibility for the spirituality, made over the revenues to a monastery, which became responsible for maintaining the parish. The monastery thus became the rector or parson and had to supply a vicar (a word which means taking the place of the parson). The procedure was that the monastery presented the vicar to the bishop, who then collated him (conferred the benefice).[10]

The lion's share of the income went to the monastery, much less to the vicar, though the monastery had responsibility for the fabric and other obligations. In the fourteenth century, in some parishes, the vicar's share was also made over to the monastery, in which case the vicar got what the monastery gave him and was termed a vicar-pensioner. The system in effect meant that underpaid vicars were doing the parish work; or even worse, that curates living at subsistence level did the work for absentee vicars. Uplifting rents and tithes from distant parishes was difficult, which led to monasteries leasing or farming out the parish revenues to laymen.[11] The monastery got ready money trouble-free, the middleman uplifted as much as he could.

This was perhaps the biggest single cause for the poor state of the medieval Church in Scotland. Institutions – not only monasteries but also cathedral chapters, collegiate churches or university colleges – got most parish revenues, while the ordinary parishioners were neglected by ill-paid, unsuitable curates. It comes across that medieval people looked on a church appointment simply as a source of income; this applies to everyone, from kings, nobles, bishops and abbots down. The idea of service and responsibility, with of course honourable exceptions, was very weak. Not only was pastoral care lacking, but the very concept of pastoral care did not seem to exist. As for using endowments for a purpose not intended by the original benefactor, not only was this commonly done but the notion that perhaps it should not be done was entirely lacking. Nowadays one would be prosecuted for maladministration of trust funds.

It can be added that monasteries, usually those of canons regular, could and did appoint a member of the community to a vicarage,[12] but sometimes this was merely an extra personal emolument and a curate did the actual parish work. For instance, the prior and the granitar of Scone held vicarages but could hardly have resided in the parishes. John Winram, later the Protestant superintendent of Fife, was vicar and then 'usufructuar' (which means he continued to enjoy the revenues after resigning) of Dull (Aberfeldy) while fully occupied as subprior of St Andrews.[13]

The fee payable to Rome on provision to a major benefice, called common services, was a single payment amounting to about a third of the monastery's annual income.[14] When Andrew Durie was provided to Melrose in 1526 he was in debt for a time, as he had had to borrow the money. When in 1541 he became bishop of Galloway, he was granted an annual pension of 1,000 marks from Melrose revenues, which was the total income of some smaller monasteries.[15] In addition to pensions given to an outgoing abbot, an unsuccessful candidate for the abbacy was often bought off with a large pension or given one as a consolation. At Arbroath in 1517, the unsuccessful James Stewart received £1,000 a year.[16] The Crown too, when nominating an abbot to Rome, sometimes awarded a large pension to a person quite unconnected with the nomination.[17]

Monasteries sometimes farmed out not only teinds and the revenues of appropriated parishes but even the monastic revenues in their entirety.[18] From 1531 on, the Crown imposed massive levies on the Church for various purposes, such as establishing the College of Justice and to meet the costs of war or embassies. Since monasteries could not pay out of income, while canon law forbade sale or alienation of church property, resort was had to granting feus, that is heritable leases, which the Crown encouraged.[19] For land that was previously leased, the new feu duty was far higher than the old rental and there was also a grassum (a down payment) to be paid on the entry of each new feuar. Clearly it was of immediate financial benefit to the monastery but there was also benefit to the feuar. As long as he paid the feu duty, he had security of tenure for himself and his heirs; there was also an unintended benefit in that the feu duty was fixed in spite of inflation. Technically a feu was not alienation, for the monastery was still the superior of the property, but it was alienation in reality, as the property could not be reclaimed unless the feuar defaulted in payment.

A feu charter therefore needed papal confirmation, but when the archbishop of St Andrews was given the powers of a legate *a latere*, which included the confirming of feu charters, they became more common. There was a great increase in the 1530s, they increased threefold in the 1540s and two and a half times again in the 1550s. For security, the feuar wanted more than a sealed document declared authentic by a notary. The communities began to sign feu charters in witness that they consented, and these signed charters are the main source for the names of monks and canons regular in the sixteenth century.

Feuing was a quick way of raising money for any purpose, including repair of buildings. Abbots also began to grant feus to their own family, often a local landed family. Church property was passing into the hands of laymen, with one unexpected result: the reformed Church after 1560 was greatly frustrated in its efforts to take over church property by these feus and by the farming out of teinds and parish revenues to laymen.

The chief criticism of feuing by monasteries is usually on social grounds. The sitting tenants, very often 'kindly' tenants (that is, tenants who were in some way kin), had no title-deeds to their land, though it was accepted that it was theirs for life and would pass to their heirs after them. If the small tenant could get a feu of his land, he had legal security and ownership *de facto*, but it cost much more, often more than he could pay. Some did manage to get the feu of their small holdings, while some had the land feued over their heads to another and were evicted by him. It has, however, been calculated by Dr Margaret Sanderson that many small sitting tenants became feuars and that there was no wholesale dispossession of small kindly tenants.[20]

Monasteries owning large tracts of land were unable by themselves to administer them and carry out the legal duties in their baronies and regalities. They therefore appointed a lay bailie, not any layman but one with sufficient power and prestige to exercise authority of himself. Increasingly this was a local lord or magnate, and increasingly the office was made hereditary.[21] In the early fifteenth century James Haldenstone, prior of St Andrews, appointed his kinsman John de Haldenstone (described as *armiger*, loosely 'gentleman') bailie for life.[22] The abbot of Newbattle in 1452 made an illicit pact appointing Sir Andrew Livingston bailie. Clearly a monastic bailiary was a desirable prize.[23]

In 1506 the abbot and community of Balmerino made Thomas Maule of Panmure the bailie of one of their baronies. His duties were to hold courts, create officers, call suits (issue summonses), administer justice, punish by fines and escheats, defend the monastery's rights and repledge (that is, transfer someone from the jurisdiction of another court to the monastery's). The bailieship became hereditary and that family became earls of Panmure.[24]

The office of bailie was granted or confirmed by charter, often explicitly as hereditary, and it gave an increase of status and even of land ownership. North of Forth, the earls of Argyll were hereditary bailies of Culross, and Ogilvies (later earls) of Airlie bailies of Arbroath and Coupar Angus.[25] In the west the earls of Cassillis were bailies of Crossraguel, and Maxwells bailies of Holywood.[26] In the Borders, as one would expect, Humes were bailies of Coldingham from 1465, and Kers bailies of Jedburgh and Kelso.[27] Most of the above were local magnates and often kin to the abbot, in fact head of the family to which the abbot belonged.

A hereditary bailie had an enormous advantage compared with an abbot, for an abbot could not have a legitimate heir, nor in Scotland could a commendator, as he had to be in major orders, which was an impediment to valid marriage.[28] In fact a commend was of its nature a one-off, an isolated appointment. Whereas an abbacy always needed a fresh election or provision, with any illegitimate son of the previous incumbent barred from succeeding, a bailieship was a lay office and could pass smoothly from father to son. Indeed, in point of time, the bailieship in a family often preceded an abbacy held by a member of that family.

It has been mentioned that the grip on a monastery was doubled if both bailie and abbot (or commendator) were of the same family. Conversely, it was a cause of strife if they were of different families and perhaps even local rivals. At Kilwinning Alexander Hamilton was abbot, while the earls of Eglinton were hereditary bailies. When two earls died in quick succession in 1545 and 1546, Hamilton tried to withhold infeftment as bailie from their successor but was obliged by a court to grant it.[29] At Glenluce two lords were bailies at different times, the earl of Cassillis and Gordon of Lochinvar, and one abbot was a Gordon. In the 1540s and 1560s there was serious strife between the two families, with the monks caught in the middle.[30]

There is always a direct correlation between the temporal administration of a monastery and its spiritual state, not so much that it affects directly the spiritual life of individual monks as that waste and inefficiency are not conducive to a healthy spiritual climate. There was an even greater correlation in an era when monks did not earn. The early Cistercians worked their land and lived on its produce, and nowadays monks can earn in diversified ways, but in late medieval Scotland the only recorded business project in which monks worked seems to have been the scriptorium at Culross.[31] When Thomas Crystal became abbot of Kinloss about 1500, he set out to reform monastic observance but also to recover monastic property and revenues encroached on by outsiders. He fought tenaciously to increase his monastery's income and thereby was able to raise the number of monks from fourteen to twenty.[32]

In Scotland, where the system of portions operated (that is, a fixed allowance to each monk for food and drink and other needs), the number of portions and thus the number of monks was directly dependent on the finances. Portions were indeed treated as tradeable assets; the canons of Inchmahome gave one for life to their secular organist, James V ordered the monks of Coldingham to give one to a secular priest, and two Cambuskenneth portions were allotted to laymen.[33] Portions could come from a specific piece of land, which probably explains the reference to 'Dene James Papis croft' at Beauly.[34] (Dene – *dompnus* in Latin – was the title given to a monk or canon regular.) No work seems to have been done on comparing the number of monks with the available monastic revenues, but the size of a community did depend directly on its income.

The evidence for communities is fragmentary and sparse apart from one source, the feu charters and precepts of sasine (instruction to give possession following on a charter) signed by the monks. Not all invariably signed and therefore, if a monk not signing is recorded or signed both before and after the charter in question, his name is to be added. The efficiency of this procedure obviously depends on the charters available; for some monasteries in some decades the documentation is good, while for other houses or at other times it is sparse.

To take the Perth charterhouse first, the complement could not exceed the twelve in the hermitages round the cloister, with perhaps prior and cellarer in the main block and a few laybrothers. There were 13 monks in 1529 and at least 11 whose careers can be followed after 1560.[35] The largest community, that of St Andrews, is poorly documented. There were over 30 canons in 1555 and 33 are recorded after 1560. Since recruitment ceased abruptly in 1560, the nine not recorded until after that date must have entered before 1560 and therefore the canons perhaps numbered 40 in the 1550s.

Numbers at Dunfermline remained steady at 25–8 between 1520 and 1560. In three monasteries, Arbroath, Lindores and Holyrood, numbers dropped slightly after the 1530s but were still over 20 in the 1550s. As for smaller monasteries, there were 18 canons at Cambuskenneth in 1445 and the same number in 1560, over a century later; at Scone 16 canons are recorded from the 1540s to the 1560s.

The Border monasteries suffered much from war and invasion. Numbers at Coldingham had risen to 11 in 1543 but there was no recruitment thereafter. At Dryburgh numbers dropped from about 18 to twelve. Jedburgh is an enigma, for never more than ten canons were recorded at any one time, though there were surely more; and only four are recorded in 1560. There was a dramatic decline at Kelso from 22 to 1540 to seven in the 1550s, though a few had perhaps gone to the priory at Lesmahagow. Probably some monks were killed in 1545 when English troops besieged the steeple with 12 monks in it and it was captured with loss of life.

Melrose suffered dramatic decline, but is puzzling. There were 35 monks in 1527, probably the largest number apart from St Andrews, but no new recruits entered until only 12 were left in 1556. At that point the community confronted their commendator, an illegimate son of James V, and succeeded in having the complement raised to sixteen. The steady decline after 1527 seems to be due to two very unsatisfactory superiors, Andrew Durie and James Stewart, rather than to the wars.

Most if not all of the small houses, Soulseat and Monymusk for instance, declined still further but there was also some growth. Two defunct monasteries, Pittenweem and Coldingham, were restored to their monastic status. Pittenweem had nine canons in the 1540s and (as said above) Coldingham reached a total of 11, while at Kinloss Thomas Crystal raised numbers to 20. The whole picture is anything but clear; it differs from region to region, from large monasteries to small ones, from one house to another. That, however, is how it was. Generalisations that have been made are not supported by the evidence.

It is clear, despite the incomplete evidence, that recruitment continued in the dozen years before 1560. Nine entered at St Andrews in the 1550s, nine at Lindores, and up to nine at Whithorn. Seven make their first appearance at Coupar Angus in the 1550s, and five at Arbroath. At Melrose five entered after 1556; at Holyrood three first appear in the late 1550s.

It also seems clear that numbers were greater than are recorded in the surviving feu charters. Monks are often recorded for the first time after 1560, at St Andrews and Lindores for example, but must have entered monastic life before then. Monks not recorded in monastic documents or found signing feu charters come to light in other documents. Such are three early Protestants, Robert Richardson and Robert Logie at Cambuskenneth and John McBrair at Glenluce.[36] An otherwise unknown canon of Cambuskenneth fought on the Queen's side at Langside in 1568. John Thomson, monk of Dunfermline, comes to light in the Acts of Parliament, and John Hume, canon of Jedburgh, in a royal letter. The record of John Mason's death in 1565 reveals him as a monk of Lindores.[37]

At Kinloss only nine monks are recorded after 1560 but 14 obviously resident monks (excluding the minister John Philip) were receiving their portion in 1574. Ferrerio's chronicle of Kinloss reveals a novice not persevering, a monk dying young, one living abroad and a laybrother not signing, all within a limited period.[38] The conclusion, albeit tentative, must be that there were many more monks and canons than have had their names recorded.

We would of course like to know more about these monks than merely their names, for instance, their age, background, education, character and so on. As usual there are odd indications here and there, with Ferrerio fleshing the picture out to some degree at Kinloss. Most indications are that recruits entered at the age of seventeen or eighteen. Thomas Crystal showed promise as a schoolboy at Culross and was therefore poached by the abbot of Kinloss. John Cameron (Capronius in Ferrerio's renaissance Latin) entered Kinloss as a boy well grounded in the humanities. The musician Robert Carver entered Scone at an early age; another musician, Andrew Blackhall, born in 1536, signed a Holyrood document in 1558.[39] On the other hand, before entering at Kinloss, James Porter was a priest, and Adam Elder a graduate of Paris, as was Thomas Hamilton of Coupar Angus. Thomas Forret, the Protestant martyr, graduated at Cologne before entering at Inchcolm. John Law, a graduate of Paris, was schoolmaster in Ayr before becoming a canon at St Andrews.[40] Robert Richardson thought no novice should be received before his eighteenth year unless one was sure of his character and his constancy. Henry Abercromby surely entered Scone at an early age, for by 1570 he had been fifty years in the community and prior for the last twenty-two, and he was to enjoy his vicarage revenues for another seven.[41]

The three John Hamiltons at Paisley were respectively from Glasgow, Bathgate and Linlithgow;[42] since the latter two places are a good distance from Paisley, one can surmise that they found their way to Paisley because John Hamilton was its abbot. Thomas Crystal, later abbot of Kinloss, was (as said above) from Culross. Much evidence, however, points to monks being local men.[43] The names are often local ones, especially in the Border abbeys. In burgh records, notary's protocol books and the like, it is striking how often monks and townspeople have the same names. One also finds explicit references to monks being related to a local burgess or indweller; it can be said with certainty that some monks or canons of St Andrews, Dunfermline, Paisley and Arbroath were local men. The widest travelled seem to have been from Edinburgh and Leith, for seven such are found respectively at Lindores, Jedburgh, Glenluce, Whithorn (two), Paisley and Deer.[44]

As for social class, almost all the relevant documents concern property on a modest scale coming to monks from a kinsman. Half of them reveal a burgess family, though there are frequent references to relatives who were tradesmen such as plumbers, builders, cordiners. One might wonder why, in a predominantly rural society, the references are so urban. Probably the land of 'kindly' tenants was passed on without documentation to a relative who would work the land rather than to a monk who was next of kin.

Relationships, to secular priests for instance, sometimes emerge without any reference to property or background. Ferrerio reveals that Robert Donaldson and Abbot Robert Reid at Kinloss and John Shanwell, abbot of Coupar Angus, were related; all were Cistercians. Even more interesting, Robert Richardson (Cambuskenneth), Alexander Alane (St Andrews), John McBrair (Glenluce) and John Bigholm (Jedburgh) were kinsmen.[45] Three of the four were canons regular and all but Bigholm were early Protestants.

It is noteworthy, in the wealth of detail given by Ferrerio – in typical schoolmasterly fashion he records the academic ability of his pupils at Kinloss – he describes Thomas Crystal as of decent stock (*honesto loco*) and from a quite old family but never once mentions a noble or landed family. We must abandon the myth of younger sons from well-to-do families drifting into an undemanding life. The monasteries recruited mostly teachable youngsters of average social standing, with a sprinkling of older literate men.

Four men of noble family entered monasteries as ordinary monks or canons and not after appointment as abbots. These were John Maxwell at Whithorn, an illegitimate son of Maclean of Urquhart at Iona, John Hamilton, illegitimate son of the earl of Arran, at Kilwinning, Adam Stewart, illegitimate son of James V, at Perth charterhouse. The first three became abbots and perhaps were destined for it, but Stewart was not destined to be a superior, for the Carthusians appointed their priors on merit alone and deposed them without hesitation. The fact that Stewart called himself prior after 1560 means nothing.

Eight men emerge as belonging to laird's families: Thomas Forret at Inchcolm; John Annand and John Winram at St Andrews; John Durie, later minister in Edinburgh, and William Lumsden at Dunfermline; John Philip, later abbot, at Lindores; Gilbert Brown at Sweetheart;[46] Adam Forman, the last Carthusian prior at Perth. Six were from Fife, of whom four became actively Protestant while three remained staunch

Catholics. It can be mentioned, without claiming any specific relevance, that Fife and the laird class tended to support the Protestant Reformation.

In sixteenth-century Scotland, when a monk made his perpetual profession and was ordained priest, he was hardly likely ever to become an abbot or autonomous prior. Lesser offices, however, were open to him. In abbeys the second-in-command was the prior and in larger houses there was also a subprior. If the monastery was a priory, the second-in-command was the subprior. At St Andrews, a large cathedral priory, there was not only a subprior but also a 'third prior' (*tertius prior*) and even, at times at least, a 'fourth prior'.[47] When the superior was absent or if he was, for instance, an under-age commendator, the second-in-command was the effective local superior; such was the official position of the prior of Paisley until the teenage John Hamilton was old enough to take over the abbacy himself.[48]

The whole subject is complex, and even as regards the common traditional monastic offices there were variations between houses. At Jedburgh in its later days, for instance, there does not seem to have been a prior but only a subprior.[49] A man with musical ability in charge of the monastic choir was termed precentor or cantor (the modern choir-master); his deputy was the *succentor*. The sacrist or sacristan took charge of the sacristy and church. There were revenues attached to the offices of precentor and sacrist at St Andrews. At Dunfermline in the fifteenth and sixteenth centuries the sacrist was provided by Rome and paid annates, the tax for minor benefices.[50] Revenues from a piece of land would be allotted to him for expenses. No doubt this was due to some dispute in the past in which one party petitioned Rome, but such an arrangement was very harmful to the ethos of monastic life. In a fair number of monasteries, if the parish church was part of the monastic church or very near, one of the community was the vicar responsible for services. At Dunfermline and Coldingham the sacrist was also vicar.[51] In many houses an elemosinar or almoner took charge of alms and dole for the poor. A novice-master undertook the training of the young monks; an infirmarian took care of the elderly and infirm monks.

As for the temporalities within the monastery, larger houses would have a cellarer and a bursar, while in smaller houses one man would undertake the duties of both. Most probably the bursar looked after the revenues and the cellarer took care of the practical aspects. Temporalities outwith the monastery were more complex; officials probably differed from one house to another and their duties developed with the passage of time. The terrarer (*terrarius*) was the equivalent, outside, of the bursar and/or cellarer. The granitar or granger collected the grain rent. There was a master of works, some Cistercian monasteries had a warden, at Melrose and some other monasteries there was a collector. The duties of these officials are not clear, nor is it always easy to distinguish an official position from a job description. This is so with Ferrerio's list of Kinloss monks under Abbots Crystal and Reid, and with titles like 'keeper of coningar' (rabbit warren) at Coupar Angus.[52] In the sixteenth century, too, laymen undertook duties formerly carried out by monks. The chamberlain, the chief financial officer who saw to collecting the rents and handled the income, was usually a layman. This official at Lesmahagow in 1557 could not write, which led Dr Coulton to judge wrongly that he was an illiterate monk. At Jedburgh and Inchaffray, on the other hand, the chamberlain was a monk.[53]

In most monasteries the monks were outnumbered by others. In the church, especially if it was large and in a town, secular priests were chaplains of altars and chapels, there were bellringers, a parish clerk and, at Paisley at least, choir boys. As for servants, information is fragmentary but there was a barber at Balmerino, a 'maister cuik' and a 'maister baxter' at Pluscarden; often there were a porter or janitor and a gardener.[54] Servants may have been plentiful, whether for the aged monks, some officials and perhaps others, or merely with general duties.

A regality needed officials, notaries and other workers. The Register of Coupar Angus shows the complexity of administering wide tracts of land, with a pyramid of responsibility in which the administration comes across as enlightened in its requirements and sympathetic in its care for tenants, especially children and the elderly.[55] Around a monastery in a town were all kinds of tradesmen, from masons and smiths to tailors and brewers, whether they worked for the monastery alone or also served the wider community. The original purpose of monastic life was to remove oneself from worldly affairs, but in late medieval Scotland the monk found himself at the nerve-centre of a very busy world.

NOTES

1. *MRHS*, pp. 245–6 and passim. These are figures estimated for 1561, given here in round numbers.
2. *St A. Form.*, i, pp. 169–70; Sanderson, 'Aspects' p. 90.
3. Sanderson, *Mary Stewart's People*, p. 105; *Newbattle Reg.*, p. xxvi; *Crossraguel Chrs*, i, pp. lx–lxi; *CSSR*, i, p. 222.
4. Lib. III, Cap. XI (fo. xlviii verso); *A History of Greater Britain*, ed. A. Constable (SHS 1892), pp. 137–8.
5. T. B. Franklin, *A History of Scottish Farming* (Edinburgh, 1952), p. 89. For the farming background, see this work and J. A. Symon, *Scottish Farming, Past and Present* (Edinburgh, 1959). For the sixteenth century in particular, see n. 19.
6. Sanderson, *Mary Stewart's People*, p. 115; 'Mauchline', pp. 93–4; *RPC* 2nd Ser., i, p. cxiv.
7. Patrick, *Statutes*, pp. 181–2; Winning, 'Church Councils', p. 354.
8. Cowan, 'Appropriation', pp. 203–22; Dowden, *Medieval Church*, pp. 113–17.
9. Cowan, *Parishes*, pp. 213–26 and passim; Cowan, 'Ayrshire Abbeys', p. 269; *Wigt. Chrs*, p. 17.
10. *Cambusk. Reg.*, nos 135, 140–1; *Beauly Chrs*, pp. 101–5, 167–8.
11. Dowden, *Medieval Church*, pp. 124–6.
12. Cowan, 'Appropriation', pp. 216–18; Haws, *Parish Clergy*, passim. See also pp. 70–1 below.
13. *Laing Chrs*, p. 410; Haws, *Parish Clergy*, pp. 168, 201; *RSS*, iv, no. 879; *RMS*, iv, no. 1730.
14. *ACSB*, p. xli.
15. Sanderson, 'Mauchline', p. 94; *Melrose Recs*, iii, pp. 202–16; *St A. Form.*, ii, pp. 137–9.
16. *St A. Form.*, i, pp. 49–51, 126; ii, pp. 139–43; *Vet. Mon.*, no. 926.
17. *St A. Form.*, ii, pp. 79–81, 183–8; *James V Letters*, passim.
18. *ADCP*, p. lvi and passim; *RSS*, ii, no. 3135.
19. For the taxation see Reid, 'Clerical Taxation', pp. 129–53; Easson, 'Reformation', pp. 11–12. The operation and effects of feu-farming are described in the various works of Dr Sanderson: 'Aspects'; 'Kilwinning'; 'Feuars'; 'Kirkmen'; 'Mauchline'; *Rural Society*; *Mary Stewart's People*, pp. 109–11.
20. See in particular Sanderson, 'Aspects', pp. 87–8; 'Kilwinning', p. 108; 'Feuars', pp. 117–24, 136; 'Kirkmen', pp. 40–1; *Mary Stewart's People*, p. 110.
21. Sanderson, *Rural Society*, pp. 24–5; Easson, 'Reformation', pp. 12–13.
22. *St A. Cop.*, pp. liv, 45–6.
23. *CPL*, x, pp. 570–1.
24. *Registrum de Panmure*, ed. J. Stuart (Edinburgh 1874), ii, pp. 269–70, 279–80, 309, 316.
25. Douglas, 'Culross', pp. 93–4; *Arbroath Lib.*, ii, passim; *C. A. Chrs*, ii, passim.
26. *Crossraguel Chrs*, i, pp. 102–5; Fergusson, 'Last Monks', p. 59; *St A. Form.*, i, pp. 78–9.
27. *RMS*, ii, nos 859, 2162; SRO, GD 40/7/4, 10; Morton, *Monastic Annals*, p. 24; Dilworth, 'Border Abbeys', p. 239.
28. Dilworth, 'Commendator System', pp. 59–61.
29. Easson, 'Reformation, p. 20; Cowan, 'Monastic Ideal', pp. 31–2; Sanderson, 'Kilwinning', pp. 82, 84; 'Kilwinning Collections', pp. 197–202.

30. Henry, 'Glenluce', pp. 139–47, 157–76; McRoberts, 'Material Destruction', p. 449.
31. Forbes, *Kalendars*, pp. xx–xxi; Ross, 'Religious Orders', pp. 215–16.
32. Ferrerius, *Historia*, pp. 66–70.
33. Durkan, 'Education', p. 149; *St A. Form.*, ii, pp. 189–93; Easson, 'Reformation', p. 20n.
34. Sanderson, *Mary Stewart's People*, p. 107; *Kinloss Recs.* 93.
35. The evidence for numbers in each house and recruitment in the 1550s is found in Dilworth's articles: 'Monks and Ministers' for the Charterhouse, Dunfermline, Arbroath, Coupar Angus, Coldingham, Melrose, Lindores; 'Border Abbeys' for Dryburgh, Jedburgh, Kelso, Melrose; 'Canons' for St Andrews, Holyrood, Cambuskenneth, Scone, Dryburgh, Jedburgh, Soulseat, Monymusk, Pittenweem; 'Dependent Priories' for Monymusk, Pittenweem; 'Augustinian Chapter', pp. 26–7 for St Andrews; 'Coldingham', pp. 133–7 for Coldingham; *Whithorn*, pp. 8–10 for Whithorn.
36. Richardinus, *Commentary*, pp. 1, 127; Durkan, 'Local Heretics', p. 27.
37. *RSS*, vi, nos 283, 863; *APS*, ii, p. 366; *James V Letters*, p. 189; *RSS*, v, no. 2265.
38. Ferrerius, *Historia*, pp. 37–8, 95–6; *Kinloss. Recs*, p. 154.
39. Ferrerius, *Historia*, pp. 35, 41, 61–3; *DSCHT* 141; Laing, 'Scottish Psalter', pp. 454–8; SRO, RH 6/1749A.
40. Ferrerius, *Historia*, pp. 38, 41; Durkan, 'Education', p. 157; id., 'Cultural Background', p. 320; id., 'Law Chronicle', p. 49; *ESL*, p. 112.
41. Richardinus, *Commentary*, p. 88; *Scone Lib.*, pp. 210–12; SRO, RH 6/1442; *RSS*, vii, nos 1032–3.
42. Durkan, 'Paisley', p. 119.
43. Dilworth, 'Social Origins', pp. 202–9. Further references are supplementary.
44. See also SRO, NP 1/196 (Prot. Bk. Robert Lausoun) fo. 62; *Protocol Book of John Foular*, ed. W. Macleod and M. Wood (SRS 1930–53), iv, p. 20; Dilworth, *Whithorn*, p. 10.
45. Durkan, 'Cultural Background', p. 297.
46. Dilworth, 'Gilbert Brown', pp. 153–4.
47. Dilworth, 'Augustinian Chapter', p. 25; Herkless and Hannay, *St Leonard*, p. 205.
48. Lees, *Paisley*, App. N.
49. NLS, MS 2100, fo. 99v.
50. *RMS*, iv, no. 1917; *CPL*, xiii, pp. 577, 834; *ACSB*, pp. 192, 205; Public Record Office 31/9/32, fo 114.
51. Cowan, *Parishes*, pp. 33, 52. For vicars and elemosinars see pp. 69–71 below.
52. SRO, CH 8/18, fo 5v; Ferrerius, *Historia*, pp. 37–8; *C. A. Rent.*, i, pp. 194–6; ii, p. 183.
53. Sanderson, *Rural Society*, pp. 24–8; Dilworth, 'Literacy', p. 71; SRO, GD 40/1/192, 200. Cf. Knowles, *Religious Orders*, ii, pp. 312ff.
54. Durkan, 'Paisley', pp. 113–19; Fleming, *Reformation*, p. 545; Macphail, *Pluscardyn*, p. 256.
55. *C. A. Rent.*, i, pp. 139–40; ii, p. 53; index s. v. Children.

# PLATES

Although originally Valliscaulian, *Pluscarden Priory* became a Benedictine house in 1454. It enjoys the unique distinction of being the only medieval monastery in Britain or Ireland that is a monastery in our time also.

*Beauly Priory*, in the eastern Highlands, was one of the very few Valliscaulian houses outside France. In its later years it was ruled by the Cistercian abbots of Kinloss (Moray).

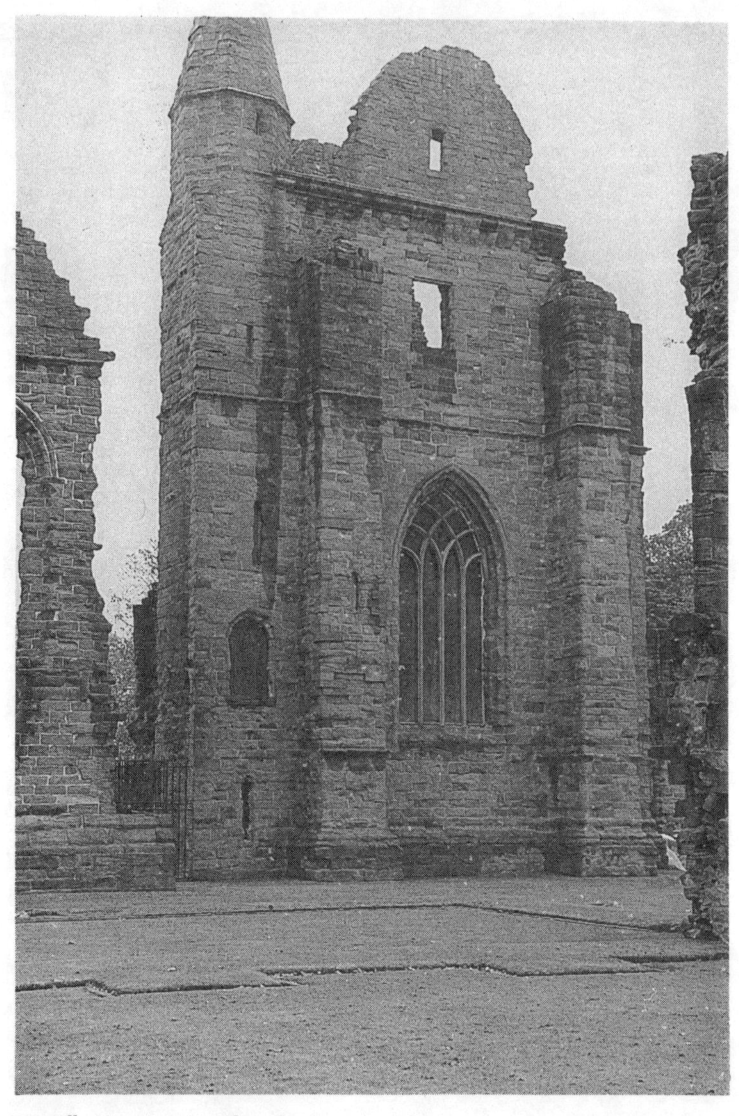

Originally Tironensian, *Arbroath* was one of the greatest Benedictine monasteries in Scotland. The celebrated 'Declaration of Arbroath' in 1320 proclaimed Scotland's status as an independent kingdom.

*Culross*, on the Fife coast, was Cistercian. In the late Middle Ages its well-known scriptorium produced fine manuscript volumes. The little town of Culross still has many medieval buildings, providing a beautiful setting for the impressive abbey remains.

Thanks to its situation on an island in the Firth of Forth, Augustinian *Inchcolm* is the best preserved of all the Scottish medieval monasteries. It was, however, vulnerable to attack from the sea during the wars with England and at times the monks had to leave the island. The photographs show the church and the refectory, the two chief focal points of monastic common life.

*Dunfermline* ranks among the great abbeys of Europe, both for its prestige and for its buildings. Its founder, the saintly Queen Margaret, was buried in the church, which became a popular place of pilgrimage. Dunfermline succeeded Iona as the burial place of Scottish sovereigns, and its royal connections continued even after the Reformation.

The Border abbeys, one from each of the four main monastic orders, formed a remarkable group. *Jedburgh* (Augustinian) was the most southerly. It suffered much in the wars with England and its later history is obscure.

Another Border abbey, *Dryburgh*, was perhaps the most important of the Premonstratensian houses, rivalled only by the cathedral priory at Whithorn. It too suffered much from war and invasion.

Many important monastic houses were located in the extreme south-west of Scotland. *Glenluce* was one of the three Cistercian abbeys there. In the decades before the Reformation it headed a sustained Cistercian effort to reform monastic observance.

*Crossraguel*, in Ayrshire, was Cluniac and was also an abbey, a rare combination in the Middle Ages. Though never large, it offered considerable resistance to the Protestant Reformation.

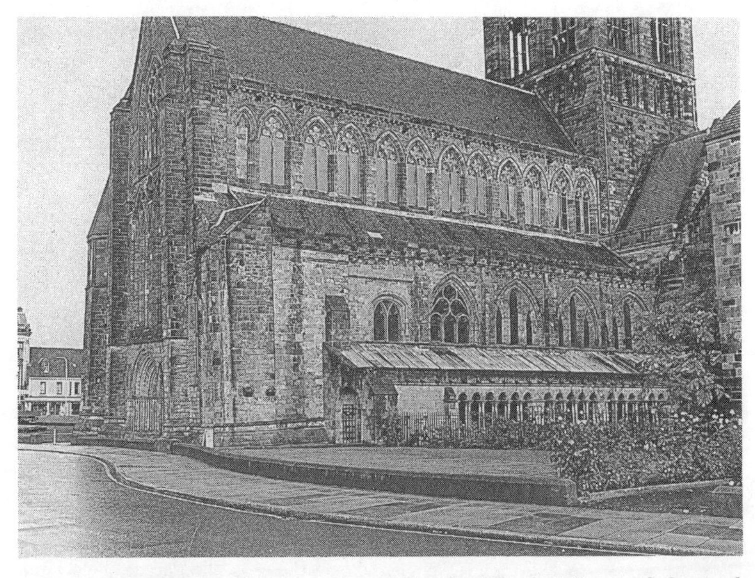

*Paisley*, also a Cluniac abbey, was associated with William Wallace and the royal Stewart dynasty and enjoyed great prestige. Although, under its Hamilton abbots, it resisted the Reformation, its great church is still used regularly for worship as a Protestant parish church.

# 5

# *Monasteries in the Life of the Country*

The place of the monasteries in the life of the nation, the Church and the particular locality can hardly be exaggerated. To begin with, they owned so much land. At a very rough estimate, half the land in Scotland belonged to the Church and half of this belonged to the monasteries.[1] In the St Andrews *Formulare*, a collection of documents assembled as a guide for the business affairs of the archbishop of St Andrews, the primate of Scotland, one fifth of them concern monasteries. Because of their wealth the monasteries had great importance as landlords and employers and dominated the economy in their locality, and this was so despite the losses caused by feuing and taxation. Two monasteries, St Andrews and Whithorn, had the added prestige of being cathedral priories playing a significant role in the affairs of the diocese. Of these, St Andrews in particular enjoyed great prestige, being the cathedral church of the most important diocese in Scotland and having, since 1512, the university college of St Leonard within its precinct.

Most abbots and both cathedral priors had the privilege of *pontificalia*, that is of using the episcopal insignia of mitre, crozier, pectoral cross and ring, and presiding at liturgical ceremonies as a bishop would.[2] This prestige was enjoyed by abbots of relatively humble background, such as Robert Forester, abbot of Balmerino 1511–61, who was (as far as we know) a monk before his elevation.[3] Much greater was the prestige of abbots from powerful local families and even from great noble houses, some of them kinsmen of the king. Such were the

Hamilton abbots of Paisley, Arbroath and Kilwinning.[4] Two of the regents who ruled Scotland during the infancy of James VI had headed monasteries before 1560.[5] Abbacies were often held by the highest churchmen in the land. Each archbishop of St Andrews and Glasgow was a commendator, holding at times between them Dunfermline, Arbroath, Paisley and Inchaffray, while the only cardinal, David Beaton, held Arbroath.[6]

Numerous abbots were important and influential office-bearers in the land, whether they were abbots promoted to the office or office-bearers given abbacies as a reward, or as sustenance, or to enhance their prestige. Abbots were often the Lord High Treasurer, the Chancellor or the King's Secretary; in particular, abbots of Dunfermline, Coupar Angus, Paisley, Holyrood and Arbroath were Keepers of the Privy Seal. Such offices were held in addition to having a seat in Parliament and being Lords of Council.[7] Abbots, such as Thomas Erskine of Dryburgh and Robert Reid of Kinloss, were sometimes sent on embassies abroad. Alexander Myln of Cambuskenneth was the first President of the College of Justice.[8] Some held a prebend by right in various cathedral chapters, while others were given positions *ad hoc*, such as being vicar general when the bishop was absent.[9] All this added to the prestige of their monasteries, although it was hardly good for monastic life, even if some such abbots did take their monastic duties seriously.

Monasteries had great prestige as royal burial places.[10] Dunfermline had early replaced Iona in this regard. Malcolm and Margaret and their sons and other kings, including Robert the Bruce, were buried there; in fact royal tombs in Dunfermline comprised those of eight kings, five queens, six princes and two princesses.[11] Every king except James IV, whose body was taken to England from Flodden field, was buried in a monastery – and James had chosen Cambuskenneth as his last resting-place like his father before him.[12] Kings were buried in Arbroath, Melrose (which also had the heart of Robert the Bruce), Holyrood, Scone, Paisley, Cambuskenneth and the Perth charterhouse. Queens too were often interred beside their husbands in monasteries, as were other royal persons, for example members of the royal Stewart family in Paisley.[13] Bishops of Dunkeld were buried in Inchcolm.[14]

Coronations continued to take place at Scone, even after the Stone was removed to Westminster by the English invaders in 1296.

James II, however, was crowned at Holyrood and James III at Kelso. The only coronations not solemnised in a monastery were those of James V and Mary Queen of Scots, which took place in Stirling castle when they were aged seventeen months and nine months respectively.

Royal marriages were solemnised in monasteries: those of James II, James III and James IV at Holyrood and of James V at St Andrews. Kings were even born in monasteries, or more accurately in the royal palaces beside monasteries – David II and James I at Dunfermline, James II at Holyrood.

One wonders what folk memory there was of Arbroath abbey being the birth-place of the famous Declaration of 1320, which affirmed the determination of the Scottish barons to maintain the independence of Scotland, or of Paisley abbey's connection with William Wallace and Robert the Bruce, or of parliaments held at Cambuskenneth.[15] Relations of monasteries with royalty continued, too, on less formal occasions, with the king and his retinue using them as stopping-places. James IV had his chamber at Jedburgh and he and his queen went often to Whithorn on pilgrimage and visited other monasteries.[16]

Benedictine Dunfermline was of course a 'palace monastery', but it was the Augustinian houses that were most remarkable for their prestigious positions. Scone was a royal palace from ancient times, Jedburgh a royal castle, and Cambuskenneth was very near the royal castle of Stirling. Holyrood grew in prestige, with James II (1437–60) being born, married, crowned and buried there, and in 1501 the building of the magnificent new royal palace began.[17]

Iona was the burial place of the Celtic kings of Scotland until the eleventh century. Until the sixteenth century and indeed in many ways until the present day, the West Highlands and Islands had a different language and culture, different allegiances, different co-ordinates from the east and south of Scotland. Until the eighteenth century, when General Wade built his roads, the sea was not a barrier but a means of communication, and it was easier to travel from the West Highlands to Ireland by sea than to, say, Aberdeen or Edinburgh by land.

Politically, until the end of the fifteenth century the Lordship of the Isles was stronger in that region than the Scottish Crown.

Ecclesiastically, the Western Isles belonged to the diocese of Sodor, which had its cathedral in the Isle of Man but was itself in the archiepiscopal province of Nidaros (Trondhjem) in Norway. Actually, the Hebrides looked rather to Ireland than to Man or Norway. The founding members of the Benedictines in Iona, the Cistercians at Saddell and the Augustinian canons in Oronsay had almost certainly come from Ireland.

There is evidence in the late Middle Ages of Irish architectural influence, as well as of work carried out by Irish masons, at Iona, Oronsay and Ardchattan.[18] Iona abbey had been granted exemption from the jurisdiction of the bishop in Man, and in 1247 was granted exemption from attending Benedictine general chapters in Scotland because it was in the province of Norway.[19] Abbots of Iona had noble concubines, and in the early fifteenth century sons and daughters of Iona abbots had become monks in the abbey or nuns in the Augustinian nunnery there.[20] This was a far cry from the Rule of St Benedict and was possibly due to traditions going back not only to the Celtic Church but perhaps even to pre-Christian times.

The Wars of Independence had split the diocese of Sodor into its English and Scottish parts. In 1499 Iona abbey became the seat or cathedral of the bishop of the Isles, the Scottish bishop of Sodor, because the cathedral in Man was the seat of the English bishop. (This happened after the death of the previous abbot of Iona, who had presumed he would live into the sixteenth century and had a sculptured monument made for himself with his year of death carved in as 15.. with a space left for the exact year to be added – but he died in 1498.) From then on, the bishop of the Isles was *ipso facto* commendator of Iona. The monastic chapter perhaps then constituted the chapter of the diocese – it is difficult to see what other chapter there might have been[21] – but unlike St Andrews and Whithorn, in Iona the bishop and not a cathedral prior was the monastic superior. It was an anomalous situation, as was shown by the extraordinary circumstance that Farquhar Maclean, a monk of Iona appointed bishop of the Isles, became thereby commendator of the monastery in which he had been a monk.[22]

Iona shared some trends with Lowland Scotland, for two powerful families, Maclean and Campbell, were rivals for the abbacy, and the bailie was a Maclean.[23] Far from being a cultural backwater, the West

Highlands were open to renaissance influences and numbered a high proportion of graduates among the clergy. Farquhar's brother, Roderick Maclean, who also became bishop and commendator of Iona, published a volume of his own Latin verse using sixteen different metrical forms.[24] It was probably the demise of the Lordship of the Isles which led to the closure of Saddell abbey in Kintyre and to the decline of the distinctive Iona school of sculpture.[25] The West Highlands began to be integrated into the kingdom of Scotland, but the process was still in its early stages in 1560.

Iona enjoyed great prestige as the burial place of Calum Cille, St Columba. So did Dunfermline, burial place of St Margaret, and Whithorn, burial place of St Ninian, while St Andrews was notable in having relics of the apostle Andrew. Other Scottish monasteries had been founded in places already considered sacred.[26] Relics and pilgrimages were a fact of life in the Middle Ages, with visits made to sacred places for a wide variety of reasons,[27] and Scottish monasteries held an important place in this aspect of medieval life.

Making the four 'heid pilgrimages' was a common reparation for homicide, though rather surprisingly there is no certainty as to which four they were. Sir Walter Scott thought they were Scone, Dundee, Paisley and Melrose; three of these four were monasteries and perhaps it was his local patriotism which made him include Melrose, though this was in fact a place of pilgrimage.[28] Through the centuries people had come, even from abroad, to visit the shrine of the apostle in the monastic cathedral at St Andrews.[29] In 1539 James V wrote to the Pope about the other monastic cathedral at Whithorn, telling him of the constant stream of pilgrims to St Ninian's shrine and adding – a typical medieval statement – that miracles were an almost daily occurrence. James III visited the shrine, as did his queen, and James IV went almost yearly. In fact in 1503 he went twice.[30]

James IV also went to Paisley, where there was the tomb of St Mirren, together with the chapel of Our Lady of Paisley and the well of St Milburga nearby.[31] James V went to Kilwinning, presumably because of St Winning's relics,[32] and to Scone, where the head of St Fergus was venerated and miracles were claimed.[33] St Margaret was of course venerated at Dunfermline and in 1468 the sacristan was given money to keep a candle always burning beside her picture.[34] At Arbroath too were relics of a relatively recent saint, Thomas à Becket; they were in a shrine at the back of the high altar and Mass was often said there.[35] Not much seems to be recorded about Culross and St Serf, though in the early fifteenth century pilgrims visited the monastery on his feast-day and from 1420 were granted an indulgence.[36]

James V visited the Isle of May in the Forth to venerate the relics of St Adrian and his companions. The monks had left the island and were now at Pittenweem, but they supported a chaplain in May and collected for his maintenance. James gave gold to make a new reliquary and paid the smith.[37] Finally, at Lesmahagow was the shrine of St Mahago, where an ancient royal endowment provided candles and James V in 1540 gave generous donations for a reliquary. Incidentally, the popular opinion of the saint and his origin were quite erroneous, for he was not Machutus from Britanny as they thought, but Mo Fhécu from Ireland.[38]

There would be indulgences granted for visits to these shrines, with processions and celebrations on the saint's feast-day. The monasteries clearly played a part in the devotional life of the people of Scotland and thereby enhanced their own prestige considerably. They also had great prestige through their impressive, even magnificent, buildings. Melrose had a large, elaborate church and the largest monastic west wing in Europe. St Andrews church, with an interior length of 357 feet, was among the largest cathedrals in Europe. Dunfermline could bear comparison with any abbey. Paisley abbey's precinct wall, up to three kilometres long, was one of the wonders of Europe.[39] The Spanish ambassador, reporting to his king in 1498, spoke of the magnificent monastic churches in Scotland and his sentiments were echoed by a French traveller in 1552. It is evident too that the furnishings and gear in the churches matched the fabric in splendour.[40]

Monasteries also played an important and prestigious part in commerce and the administration of justice.[41] Their land holdings were large enough to be baronies (a barony being the local unit of rural life) and as such had their own mill, fixed prices and regulated the management of land. Their trading centre was the burgh of barony, with privileges of holding a market, a court and an annual fair. By 1400 there were eight such burghs, the abbot being the baron, and their number grew steadily. Newburgh was the burgh of Lindores, Canongate (separate from Edinburgh) that of Holyrood.

A much more important unit was the lordship or regality, for the lord had almost royal jurisdiction (hence the term 'regality'). He could judge the four pleas, that is murder, fire-raising, rape and robbery, in fact every crime except treason. The king's writ did not run in a regality, and the king's officer could be excluded; the tenants of the regality could be repledged to its court from a royal justice ayre (circuit), for the lord could insist on dealing with his delinquents himself. The lands of all the important monasteries were regalities, as were those of many monasteries of second rank, such as Crossraguel, Newbattle, Kinloss.

Baronies making up a regality could be distant from each other. There is, for instance, much in Ferrerio's chronicle about Kinloss's barony of Strathisla in upper Banffshire, whereas Kinloss was on the Moray coast. Dunfermline's regality had four burghs, Musselburgh, Kirkcaldy, South Queensferry and Dunfermline itself, and also lands in Moray with the dependent priory of Urquhart and later of Pluscarden. A regality needed officials, notaries, a chancery and all the rest, which is no doubt why the abbot of Arbroath was given authority in 1425 to enrol six notaries.[42] The monk Ralph Hudson was scribe and notary in the court of Melrose.[43] Monasteries in fact played a very important and prestigious role in the administration of affairs and of justice in large tracts of land and a fair number of towns.

As regards level of education and culture, we must abandon two mutually exclusive stereotypes: that the monks were uncouth and illiterate, and that they spent their day in the scriptorium copying and illuminating manuscripts. Dr Coulton showed a healthy scepticism about the latter – perhaps even over-reacted – but was too ready to accept alleged instances of illiteracy.[44] The evidence for a reasonable level of literacy is in fact overwhelming. In St Benedict's Rule reading was an important and integral part of monastic life. There were readings in the choir office (Chapters 9, 11); the monks took their turn at reading aloud during meals (Chapter 38); part of each day was allotted to reading privately and each monk was given a book from the library to read during Lent (Chapter 48); a lengthy reading preceded Compline to give time for all the brethren to assemble (Chapter 42). A monk without Latin or unable to read was of limited use in the community, and if books were so necessary, they had to be readily available. In the first half of the sixteenth century, too, renaissance influence was powerful and books became more available because of printing. Scotland at the time was characterised by a vigorous regard for university education and a remarkably high level of achievement in literature and music.

The thousands of signatures on the feu charters and precepts of sasine signed by monks do not look semi-literate. Out of all these, only two exceptions have come to light. A monk of Iona in 1532 signed *tenta penna*, which means that a notary signed for him. In 1555 a notary signed for John Rig, a canon of Whithorn, stating that the latter could not write; but later documents have Rig's scrawled signature, showing that he was learning.[45] Every other claim that a monk was unable to write has been found to be erroneous. It therefore seems likely that the monk of Iona was unable to write because he had gone blind, or sprained his wrist, or some such reason. Nuns in Scotland commonly could not write, but that is another story: the education of women in a male-dominated society.[46] Monks had at least a reasonable level of literacy in both Latin and the vernacular. Indeed many monastic officials had to write and keep accounts, and monks were notaries in at least five monasteries: Ralph Hudson at Melrose, as mentioned above; Robert Williamson at Lindores; John Westwater at Culross; Silvester Ireland at Coupar Angus; John Henryson at Dunfermline.[47]

When the Perth charterhouse was founded, the monks brought manuscript volumes with them from the Continent and borrowed others in Scotland, their intention being to copy them in order to build up a library of their own and then return the volumes to the lenders. One monk made a copy of Barbour's *Bruce* and Blind Harry's *Wallace*.[48] There are references to monks scribing at Kinloss, Newbattle and Dunfermline, and even as late as 1554 at Pittenweem. Culross had a well-known scriptorium which apparently operated commercially.[49] In the first half of the sixteenth century there was a certain role for copying texts, but a diminishing one because of the steadily increasing amount of printed material becoming available.

The losses suffered by Scottish medieval libraries have been enormous – in fact it can be said that survivals are accidental – but all the indications are that monasteries had large libraries. A specialist writer concludes that Scottish monastic libraries were as large as those in English houses and that 'Scottish monasteries were in no respect less well-equipped with libraries than English houses'. To quote just one fact, Jedburgh had sixty-nine works by St Augustine.[50] Arbroath in 1517 had over 200 volumes (which seems an understatement).[51] At Kinloss Abbot Crystal obtained a range of volumes for the library, and his successor, Robert Reid, not only built up a collection of books on all subjects but erected a stone building for them, with precautions against fire.[52] The work on surviving volumes by the late Neil Ker and by Dr John Durkan points to Scottish monasteries having fair holdings of manuscript and printed works.[53]

Volumes with a Scottish provenance are sometimes found abroad.[54] An interesting episode occurred in 1553 when Marcus Wagner came to Scotland searching for historical material.[55] He visited St Andrews, Arbroath, Coupar Angus, Scone and Cambuskenneth, taking manuscript volumes from the first three away with him, and noted that he saw volumes of unusual age and beauty to which there was nothing comparable in Germany, Italy or Denmark. At St Andrews he saw volumes in corners, exposed to vermin and damp; from what we know of St Andrews at the time, they were surely discarded volumes not in demand.

Some men who were already graduates of Cologne, Paris and St Andrews became monks, and some who were already monks were sent to universities in Scotland and abroad. As we have seen, Alexander Myln sent young canons of Cambuskenneth to Paris; monks of Kilwinning went to Glasgow university, canons of St Andrews made use of the facilities on their doorstep.[56] The reform movements at Cambuskenneth, St Andrews and Kinloss involved the raising of educational standards. Two Kinloss monks were sent to study with the Dominicans in Aberdeen, and the young monks at Kinloss and Beauly received a sound education from the scholar in residence, Ferrerio.[57]

A monk of Dunfermline, James Reydpeth, inscribed two books with his name in Latin elegiac couplets, with the hexameter different in each. Not much is known of how widespread was any knowledge of Greek at this time in Scotland, though among those credited with knowing it were Alexander Alane (Alesius), Robert Richardson, Adam Elder at Kinloss and Robert Stephenson at Deer. One amusing instance of at least a nodding acquaintance with the language is provided by David Bowok at Glenluce, who in 1547 added the pidgin Greek *policronitudo basileos* ('multi-time-ness of a king' – really just nonsense) to his signature on a feu charter. Ten years later he added *more solito* (meaning roughly 'as usual') on another feu charter.[58] One wonders if he was simply a humorist or letting it be known that he considered signing the charters a mere charade.

No great works of literature or erudition were written by monks but they did compile chronicles. Two are very well known, and are in fact major sources for the history of Scotland: Andrew Wyntoun's chronicle in verse and Walter Bower's continuation of the *Scotichronicon*. A monk of Perth charterhouse produced a shortened version of the *Scotichronicon* because of its *tediosa prolixitas*.[59] John Law of St Andrews and John Smith of Kinloss compiled chronicles on a narrower scale.[60] Robert Richardson (Cambuskenneth) had his *Exegesis* printed at Paris, a by no means handsome little volume, very unlike the *Chapter Discourses* of Adam Elder (Kinloss), elegantly produced at Paris even if the contents are not very memorable.[61]

The reforming church councils of 1549–59 issued decrees about the teaching of theology and scripture in monasteries. Qualified men were at once to begin teaching and preaching, and the commendator, George Durie, arranged for a Dominican friar to do this at Dunfermline. Each monastery was also to send monks to university to study scripture and theology for four years; in fact the 1549 council laid down the number for each house.[62] Since the evidence is so fragmentary, it is impossible to judge to what extent these measures were necessary. No doubt in some monasteries they were. Granted that the monasteries produced no outstanding scholar – the theologian Quintin Kennedy at Crossraguel was not a monk before being provided as abbot – the level of study at St Andrews and Kinloss was undoubtedly high and we can tentatively conclude that in other houses it was average, with a reasonable spread of ability and achievement.

The isolated references to arts and crafts do not amount to much. The scriptorium at Culross produced illuminated manuscripts and fine binding. A monk of Kilwinning built an organ in Ayr and he or a fellow-monk bound books. Monks of Lindores and Culross worked for

James IV as masters of works at Stirling castle and the palaces at Falkland and Linlithgow. Culross and Kinloss were known for their gardens; Robert Reid brought a gardener from Normandy and a painter of pictures to Kinloss.[63] And of course various practical skills were needed in the complex structure of a large monastery, though no notable talent is recorded.

There is, however, no need to make guarded statements about music in the monasteries. One of the most interesting developments in recent Scottish historical studies has been the realisation that in the first half of the sixteenth century the standard of music was as high in Scotland as anywhere in Europe.[64] Recent work on a manuscript from Inverness has revealed remarkable polyphony being sung about 1550 in Inverness parish church and sang schule.[65] And in this brilliant context, the best practitioners were canons regular and monks.

Pride of place must go to Robert Carver (c. 1490–1566), canon of Scone, described as one of the greatest contrapuntists of his day. Among his compositions are a Mass for ten voices and a motet for no less than nineteen. His work, praised by modern musicologists for its beauty, originality and technical skill, is undergoing a revival and proving popular. David Peebles (St Andrews), called one of the principal musicians in Scotland, composed a canticle in four parts, to which a young canon added a fifth, while two other St Andrews canons were skilled musicians. Three other men were well-known musicians: John Angus (Dunfermline), Thomas Wood (Lindores), Andrew Blackhall (Holyrood).

Paisley abbey had choirboys; many, perhaps most or even all, monasteries had organs.[66] Nor was all the music solemn and church-centred. James IV on a visit to Whithorn gave money to 'twa lutars' and later to the prior's *clarsair* (harpist). He also paid for four horses to take four Italian minstrels from Whithorn to Tongland, another Premonstratensian monastery.[67]

Another stereotype or 'myth' is the identifying of medieval monasteries with education. By education is meant here instruction given to youth other than the young monks within the monastery. Certainly Scottish monasteries were involved with education to a fair extent.[68] It has to be understood, however, that there was no obligation whatsoever for a monastery or any individual monk to be involved in any good work, education included, for that was not their *raison d'être*. The same principle holds good for individual or collective talent in the arts, crafts, music and so on. If a monastery was in fact involved in any social or cultural good work, it is irrelevant (though undoubtedly interesting) whether monks or secular priests or laymen carried it out. It depended on what expertise was available.

Of Culross after 1560 it was said that there had always been a grammar school within the abbey, where the youth of the burgh and land of Culross were 'instructit in gramar and tranit in vertew'. Thomas Crystal, later abbot of Kinloss, was born in Culross, and he and his brother were taught by the monk Thomas Pearson.[69] Arbroath abbey, on the other hand, hired a graduate secular cleric in 1486 for three years to teach the novices and *juvenes confratres*, and one wonders if the latter were all aspirants to the monastic life or included youth of the neighbourhood. That particular teacher seems later to have joined the community.[70]

The picture can only be built up from the fragments of evidence that have survived. It is by the merest chance that we know of a school in 1526 at Newburgh (the burgh of Lindores, just ten to fifteen minutes' walk from the abbey). In earlier times at least, Kelso abbey conducted a school at Roxburgh and perhaps at Kelso itself, with the scholars lodged in the monastery's 'poor's house'.[71] In 1468 Dunfermline had provided a house for the schoolmaster and funds for poor scholars to be taught gratis. The poet Robert Henryson around 1500 was the chief schoolmaster, showing that there was more than one. Later, in the 1540s and 1550s, the monk John Henryson (perhaps kin to the poet) was master of the grammar school.[72]

The canons of St Andrews conducted a grammar school in their university college of St Leonard, and probably too a grammar school in the cathedral, in which they may well themselves have done the teaching.[73] The grammar school in the burgh of Canongate was under the authority of the Holyrood canons, and the abbot of Holyrood appointed the master in the High School of Edinburgh, the adjacent burgh. Paisley certainly had a grammar school before 1560, for the school begun in 1576 was a re-erection, though it was secular chaplains who did the teaching.[74]

Since the evidence is so sparse and fragmentary, it is legitimate to presume that there were other schools in monasteries or monastic burghs. A monastic lordship could contain burghs some distance away, for instance Musselburgh in the regality of Dunfermline, and it is thus very possible that the abbot of Dunfermline was the patron and provider of Musselburgh grammar school. Possibly too the same is true of parishes appropriated to a monastery, and the grammar schools of Stirling, Linlithgow and Perth had Dunfermline or St Andrews as their patron and provider. The role of the monasteries in education in the sixteenth century is largely unknown but cannot be written off as negligible.

Medieval Scotland did care for those in need. It is a complex subject, for the needs were so varied and gave rise to so many different kinds of institution, and the complexity is compounded by lack of evidence. In order to assess the role of the monasteries in this area, two observations must be made. Firstly, the word 'hospital' had a more general meaning than at the present day; it comprised what we now know as hospitals, hostels, hospices and other institutions. Secondly, only the services provided by autonomous monasteries are considered here, and thus places such as the hospital of Soutra are not included, although they were administered by Augustinians who perhaps also were termed canons.[75]

Some monasteries had a monk elemosinar (almoner) who had funds available and saw to the distribution of left-over food and also of foodstuffs and perhaps money allotted for the purpose. Certainly there was an elemosinar at Dunfermline,[76] St Andrews, Paisley and Arbroath. Some monasteries had institutions in their precinct or nearby; Dunfermline, for example, had three and there was a 'poor's infirmary' at Newbattle and almonries at Kelso, Arbroath, St Andrews and Jedburgh. Doles were given out at Dunfermline and Arbroath, to mention only two. Pluscarden distributed £41 and 40 hundredweight of victuals yearly; Lesmahagow gave out a small amount, while Paisley made a weekly distribution of very substantial amounts.[77] Monasteries were also patrons or administrators of institutes elsewhere. Dunfermline had been concerned with two in Perth, which were transferred to the charterhouse, and St Andrews had founded one in Haddington and one in Linlithgow. Holyrood continued to support St Leonard's hospital in Edinburgh.[78]

Isolated scraps of information give an indication of the range and complexity of the services provided. The abbot of Kilwinning was patron of a bed in St Giles' hospital, Edinburgh. Holyrood cared for old abbey servants, Coupar Angus showed benevolent paternalism to its tenants in need. Kinloss supported a sailor's hostel, and one of its abbots gave alms liberally to mendicant friars and supplied dowries for poor girls.[79]

The church council of 1549 ordered superiors to see that alms for the poor were given again as of old and the fabric of these caring institutions maintained.[80] The position of administrator in a hospital was considered a benefice, a source of revenue, and undoubtedly some incumbents lined their own pockets. The evidence is insufficient to assess the record of the monasteries in this regard but, as already said, medieval people had few scruples about the purpose of an endowment. St Andrews in 1512, in founding its college of St Leonard, transferred revenues given for the poor and aged to a college for poor clerks.

Canons regular and monks sometimes served in parishes.[81] In about thirty monasteries, without taking into account the non-conventual dependent priories, the monastic church served as the parish church, or the parish church was near enough to be served from the monastery. At Kelso part of the church was open to everyone at all times, whereas the part used by the monks was open to men at times of office but to women on certain feasts only.[82] In a monastic church belonging to canons, or if the nearby parish church was appropriated to them, a canon would serve as vicar and provide the parish services. In the case of monks, one cannot be so sure. At Dunfermline and Coldingham the monk sacrist was the vicar; at Lindores, Balmerino, Glenluce and Melrose the vicar was a monk. Possibly this was so at other houses, but where the vicar was not a monk a secular priest held the office, or else a monk (as at Culross) or a curate without a manse (as at Kilwinning) served the church.[83]

As for appropriated parishes distant from the monastery, monks did not serve as vicars but canons could. It was part of their ethos, though they were not supposed to do it alone but in company with fellow canons. In the sixteenth century, possibly because of decline in numbers, canons served in only a few of their appropriated churches and they served alone. Evidence for canon-vicars, as for so much else, is fragmentary but perhaps a couple of dozen canons in the decades before 1560 were vicars of parishes distant from the monastery. All the time, however, one large doubt remains about these vicars, whether they were monks or canons and whether the parish was near or far from the monastery, namely that there is no guarantee that they actually worked in the parish. It was possible to hold the title, draw the revenues and employ a curate to do the work. Monasteries in fact made only a small contribution to maintaining parish service in Scotland, but of course this was not their function anyway.

One final minor social service provided by monasteries should be mentioned: they served as a repository for valuables in the days before banks. The Perth charterhouse kept 1,000 marks for the bishop of Dunkeld, and the abbot of Crossraguel kept valuables for the archbishop of Glasgow. In 1538 the lords of session ordered restitution when 1,000 marks in gold and silver were taken from a canon's chalmer in the dortor (room in the dormitory) at Whithorn.[84] Surely that enormous sum had been deposited with the canon for safe-keeping. No doubt in other minor ways too the monasteries helped the wheels of life to go round.

## NOTES

1. I. F. Grant, *The Social and Economic Development of Scotland before 1603* (Edinburgh, 1930), p. 223 (though some figures should be taken with caution).
2. See articles on individual monasteries in *DSCHT*.
3. MRHS, p. 73.
4. Brady, *Episcopal Succession*, i, pp. 166–7, 195–6, 206–7; Lees, *Paisley*, pp. 195–6, App. N; Hannay, 'Papal Bulls', pp. 25–30; Finnie, 'House of Hamilton', pp. 8–13.
5. Dilworth, 'Border Abbeys', pp. 245–6; 'Commendator System', pp. 59–60; *DSCHT*, p. 794.
6. Dowden, *Bishops*, passim.
7. Nicholson, *Scotland*, pp. 559–60; Lynch, *Scotland*, pp. 103–4. Individuals can most conveniently be seen in the lists of witnesses in *RMS* and the sederunts in *APS* and *RPC*.
8. *St A. Form.*, ii, pp. 331–4; Ferrerius, *Historia*, pp. 40–1, 50; *DSCHT*, p. 616.
9. I. B. Cowan, 'The Organisation of Scottish Secular Cathedral Chapters', *RSCHS*, xiv (1963), pp. 34–7; *St A. Form.*, i, p. 28; ii, pp. 124–5, 199; Dilworth, 'Augustinian Chapter', pp. 20–1; Dilworth, *Whithorn*, p. 7.
10. The important royal occasions can be found in Dunbar, *Scot. Kings*. Other references are supplementary.
11. Cruden, *Medieval Churches*, pp. 35–8; NLS, MS 2101, fo 17 v.

12. *Cambusk. Reg.*, pp. cxxxii–cxxxiii.
13. Durkan, 'Paisley', pp. 110, 114.
14. *DSCHT*, p. 427.
15. Durkan, 'Paisley', p. 110; *Cambusk. Reg.*, pp. xliii–xlvi; Nicholson, *Scotland*, pp. 91–2, 114–16, 373.
16. TA, i–iv passim; *Wigt. Chrs*, p. 188.
17. *DSCHT*, p. 411.
18. I am indebted for this information to Dr Richard Fawcett.
19. *CPL*, i, pp. 231, 504.
20. *CSSR*, i, ii passim; Dilworth, 'Social Origins', pp. 197–8.
21. Dilworth, 'Iona', pp. 80–1; Watt, *Fasti*, pp. 207–8.
22. Dilworth, 'Iona', pp. 84–6.
23. *Ibid.*, pp. 78, 86–8, 97–8.
24. R. Sharpe, 'Roderick MacLean's Life of St Columba in Latin Verse', *IR*, 24 (1991), pp. 111–13.
25. K. A. Steer and J. W. M. Bannerman, *Late Medieval Monumental Sculpture in the West Highlands* (Edinburgh, 1977), p. 63.
26. The index to *MRHS* reveals a number of these.
27. *DSCHT*, p. 660. Forbes, *Kalendars* is very informative on the saints and the places where they were venerated. M. Barrett, *A Calendar of Scottish Saints* (2nd edn, Fort Augustus, 1919), summarises the information.
28. McKay, 'Heid Pilgrimages', pp. 76–7; *CPL*, vii, p. 570.
29. McRoberts, *St Andrews*, pp. 129–36.
30. TA, i, ii, iii passim; *James V Letters*, pp. 362–3; Brooke, *St Ninian*, pp. 3–6.
31. Durkan, 'Paisley', pp. 110–14.
32. TA, ii, p. 291; 'Kilwinning Collections' 120–8; Ker, *Kilwinning* 88–9.
33. TA, ii, pp. xlix, 265; iii, p. 283.
34. McRoberts, *St Margaret*, pp. 24–9; *CPL*, xii, p. 297; TA, ii, p. 267.
35. *Vet. Mon.*, no. 926.
36. *CSSR*, i, p. 208.
37. TA, vii, p. 396; *St A. Form.*, i, p. 64.
38. TA, vii, pp. 395–6; A. Boyle and M. Dilworth, 'Some Identifications of Scottish Saints', *IR*, xxxv (1984), pp. 40–1.
39. Cruden, *Medieval Churches*, pp. 28, 35, 73; McRoberts, *St Andrews*, pp. 153–4; Malden, *Paisley*, pp. 20–1.
40. McRoberts, 'Material Destruction', p. 455. See also p. 28 above.
41. There are informative accounts of baronies, burghs and regalities in *Kirkintilloch Ct. Bk*, especially pp. xi–xvii, xlii–xlviii; *Dunfermline Ct. Bk*, pp. 1–33; Sanderson, *Rural Society*, p. 6. Other references are supplementary.
42. *CPL*, vii, p. 389.
43. *Melrose Recs*, iii, pp. 149–62.
44. Coulton, *Scottish Abbeys*, pp. 157–61.
45. Dilworth, 'Iona', p. 106; Dilworth, 'Canons', p. 178.
46. Dilworth, 'Literacy', p. 72.
47. SRO, RD 1/11, fo 66; *Laing Chrs*, nos 819–970; *C. A. Chrs*, ii, pp. 148, 150, 162; Webster, *Dunfermline Abbey*, p. 86.
48. Beckett, 'Perth Charterhouse', pp. 37, 52–3, 57, 61; *St A. Cop.*, pp. 203, 482.
49. Ferrerius, *Historia*, pp. 33, 35; Ross, 'Religious Orders', pp. 215–16, 225; Durkan, 'Cultural Background', pp. 274–5.
50. McRoberts, 'Material Destruction', pp. 457–8; E. A. Savage, *Notes on the Early Monastic Libraries of Scotland* (Edinburgh, 1928), especially pp. 7–8.

51. *Vet. Mon.*, no. 926.
52. Ferrerius, *Historia*, pp. 41, 47, 77; J. Durkan, 'The Beginnings of Humanism in Scotland', *IR*, iv (1953), pp. 19–24, 119–21.
53. Ker, *Medieval Libraries*, pp. xi, 4–184; *ESL* passim, with supplements in various issues of *The Bibliotheck*; J. Durkan, 'An Arbroath Book Inventory of 1473', *The Bibliotheck*, iii (1961), pp. 144–6; *St A. Cop.*, p. 382; Sanderson, 'Kilwinning', p. 116.
54. *Dunfermline Ct. Bk*, pp. 162–3; H. M. Bannister, *Specimen Pages of Two Manuscripts of the Abbey of Coupar-Angus* (Rome, 1910); *St A. Cop.*, pp. xxxi–xxxii.
55. *St A. Cop.*, pp. xiii–xxix.
56. *ESL*, p. 112; *St A. Recs*, passim, e.g. pp. 224, 232, 239, 259; Sanderson, 'Kilwinning', p. 115; Dilworth, 'Augustinian Chapter', p. 27.
57. Ferrerius, *Historia*, pp. 41, 43–4, 49–50, 80.
58. *ESL*, p. 137 and plate XXXIII; Durkan, 'Cultural Background', p. 289; *Wigt. Chrs*, nos 55, 60, checked with originals in SRO, GD 99 (Barnbarroch).
59. D. E. R. Watt, 'Abbot Walter Bower of Inchcolm and his *Scotichronicon*', *RSCHS*, 24 (1992), pp. 286–304; Beckett, 'Perth Charterhouse', p. 37; *St A. Cop.*, pp. 203, 482.
60. Durkan, 'Law Chronicle', pp. 49–62; *Kinloss Recs*, pp. 3–13.
61. Richardinus, *Commentary* (a reprint); *Kinloss Recs*, pp. 65–91 (extracts).
62. Patrick, *Statutes*, pp. 105–7, 136, 176; Winning, 'Church Councils', pp. 339–40, 343, 351, 354–5; Ross, 'Religious Orders', p. 212; Durkan, 'Cultural Background', pp. 328–9.
63. Ross, 'Religious Orders', pp. 215–17, 224; Sanderson, 'Kilwinning', pp. 115–16; Ferrerius, *Historia*, pp. 48, 50–1. Additional references: *RSS*, i, no. 296; *TA*, i, pp. 311, 322–3, 339, 355, 368, 384.
64. D. J. Ross, *Musick Fyne: Robert Carver and the Art of Music in Sixteenth Century Scotland* (Edinburgh, 1993); *DSCHT*, pp. 16–17, 141, 650–1, 892; Durkan, 'Education', pp. 148–50; Dilworth, 'Canons', pp. 170–1. Other references are supplementary.
65. S. Allenson, 'The Inverness Fragments: Music from a Pre-Reformation Scottish Parish Church and School', *Music & Letters*, 70 (1989), pp. 1–45.
66. See for instance *Vet. Mon.*, nos 926–7; Ferrerius, *Historia*, p. 32; Durkan, 'Education', pp. 149, n. 35.
67. *TA*, ii, p. 107; iii, p. 375.
68. Easson, 'Education', pp. 13–26; Durkan, 'Education', pp. 155–68. Other references are supplementary.
69. Todd, 'Dunblane Diocese', p. 37; Ferrerius, *Historia*, pp. 61–2.
70. Durkan, 'Education', p. 161; *Arbroath Lib.*, ii, pp. 245, 316.
71. *Kelso Lib.*, p. xliii, nos 173, 409.
72. Webster, *Dunfermline*, pp. 86–8.
73. J. S. H. Burleigh, 'Scottish Reforming Councils 1549–1559', *RSCHS*, xi (1955), p. 201.
74. Durkan, 'Paisley', pp. 120–1.
75. Durkan, 'Care of Poor', pp. 116–28. A list of known hospitals is in *MRHS*, pp. 162–200. Other references are supplementary.
76. For Dunfermline see also *NLS*, Adv. 29.4.2 (vi), fos 193–4; *Dunfermline Ct. Bk*, pp. 185–92.
77. Macphail, *Pluscardyn*, pp. 255–6; *Kelso Lib.*, p. 480; Durkan, 'Paisley', pp. 116, 119.
78. J. Smith and H. M. Paton, 'St Leonards Land and Hospital', *The Book of the Old Edinburgh Club*, 23 (1940), pp. 111–46.

79. *C. A. Rent.*, ii, pp. xxi–xxiii; Ferrerius, *Historia*, pp. 78, 80.
80. Patrick, *Statutes*, pp. 119, 139–40.
81. Cowan, 'Cure of Souls', pp. 215–29. The status of each parish is given in Cowan, *Parishes* and the incumbents after 1540 in Haws, *Parish Clergy*. Other references are supplementary.
82. *Vet. Mon.*, no. 927.
83. Todd, 'Dunblane Diocese', p. 37; Sanderson, 'Manse and Glebe', p. 82.
84. Beckett, 'Perth Charterhouse', p. 38; *Crossraguel Chrs*, pp. xxxix, 108; *Wigt. Chrs*, p. 32.

# 6

# *Monasteries and the Reformation*

At the Reformation Parliament of August 1560, Catholicism was abrogated and Protestantism was made the religion of the land. The Scottish Reformation was unique in Europe in several ways. It was the last in time; or in other words, no attempt to introduce Protestantism into any country was successful after that date. It was the only exception to the adage *Cujus regio, ejus religio* ('the State religion is that of the Ruler'), for Mary Stewart, the sovereign at the time, remained a Catholic. Lastly, it was not violent, particularly where the monasteries were concerned.

Paradoxically, St Leonard's college at St Andrews played a significant part in preparing the ground for the Reformation. Although it was founded in 1512 to educate priests in austere living and academic studies, a student imbued with Reformation principles was said to have drunk at St Leonard's well. Two of its alumni became Protestants and fled the country. A canon of St Andrews, Alexander Alane, better known as Alesius ('wanderer' in Greek), fled in 1532 and his career as a Lutheran theologian in Germany and England is well known. John Fyfe, possibly also a canon, fled to Germany. On the other hand, John Annand, the canon who was first principal of the college, remained a staunch and indeed militant Catholic. In 1559–60 the staff of St Leonard's went over to the Protestant side.[1]

Cambuskenneth also played a part in preparing for the Reformation. Robert Richardson, who paradoxically had published a commentary on the Rule of St Augustine advocating a strict monastic life, went to

England and for many years was a Protestant minister. He made a brief return to Scotland in the early 1540s during Governor Arran's temporary *rapprochement* with Protestantism. Robert Logie, canon of Cambuskenneth, brother or kin to the Gavin Logie who taught Protestant doctrine at St Leonard's college, also went to Protestant England, together with Thomas Cocklaw, a priest in a parish near Cambuskenneth and perhaps also a canon. With them was associated Thomas Forret, canon of Inchcolm, who was executed for heresy at Edinburgh in 1539.[2]

A monk of Glenluce took the same path as Alesius. John McBrair, said to have been a relative of Alesius and Robert Richardson, had been a student at St Andrews, though not at St Leonard's. Around 1550 he was condemned for heresy and warded with Archbishop John Hamilton, and later had a career as a Protestant in Germany and England. The almost contemporary historian, David Calderwood, tells of a Perth Carthusian, Andrew Charters, who in 1537 fled to England, then to the Continent and from there wrote to his brother, the provost of Dundee, criticising the 'Spiritual Order' in Scotland.[3] Two canons, Donald McCarny (Holywood) and William Forman (Holyrood), were quite separately accused of heresy and agreed to toe the orthodox line,[4] but there is no evidence that they leaned towards Protestantism in any way.

An odd incident happened at Paisley in 1539. Three monks were accused of heresy, abjured and were given leave to go abroad. A novice, John Wallace, was accused of telling lies about them and was also allowed to go abroad.[5] It is worth mentioning that some well-known men who later became Protestants were judges in heresy trials not long before 1560. Such were Donald Campbell, abbot of Coupar Angus, and John Winram, subprior of St Andrews, who had taken part in the trial of Walter Milne in 1558. It has therefore been inferred that their conversion to Protestantism was late and hurried, but this was not necessarily the case, for theologians in heresy cases sat with the judges, and were called judges, but in fact were present as experts or assessors.[6]

The Reformation struggle mounted to a crisis in 1559–60. Armed bands roamed the country and church property was at risk; French troops backed the Catholics, English troops backed the Protestants. Various abbots and commendators joined the Lords of the

Congregation, the political wing of the Reformers, or declared for Protestantism: James Stewart (St Andrews), John Stewart (Coldingham), Donald Campbell (Coupar Angus), Walter Reid (Kinloss), John Philip (Lindores).[7] At St Andrews various canons declared themselves Protestants. Lindores monks were commanded to shed their 'monkish habits', while at Coupar Angus Donald Campbell put on 'secular weed' and was told by the Lords of the Congregation to destroy Catholic gear and make his monks take off their habits.[8] On the other hand, the Queen Regent stopped the portions of Cambuskenneth canons who had 'forsaken Papistry' (a most unlikely happening on the surface but in fact very possible, as a Crown appointee was administering Cambuskenneth at the time).[9]

Churches were 'cast doun', that is, purged of anything savouring of the old religion. This happened in some regions, not in others. In Fife and Tayside the monasteries of Dunfermline, St Andrews, Lindores and Coupar Angus were cast doun, possibly too Arbroath to the north; inland, Cambuskenneth, Scone and the charterhouse; in Lothian and to the south Holyrood, Kelso and perhaps Melrose; in the west Paisley, Kilwinning, Crossraguel. John Knox, describing the charterhouse as 'a building of wondrous cost and greatness', said that it was 'within two days ... so destroyed that only the walls did remain', which must have taken some doing.[10] The monks went to nearby Errol, probably to continue as best they could their closely structured life.[11]

The subsequent history of the monastic churches is outwith our purpose here, but it should be realised that destruction was by no means total.[12] The reformers naturally wanted to retain churches that were needed for parish services. At Paisley the old monastic church is still the Protestant parish church; at Monymusk and Fearn this is basically so; at Culross part of the old church remains in use and at Coldingham one old wall forms part of the structure. The nave at Dunfermline was used for Protestant worship until the nineteenth century, when a new church was built on the site of the ruined choir and sanctuary. Holyrood church was similarly used until in 1686 James VII expelled the Protestant worshippers to make way for a Jesuit college and built Canongate kirk for them.[13]

Various other monastic churches remained for a long time in use, some until the nineteenth century: Kelso, Melrose and Jedburgh in the Borders; Whithorn, Dundrennan and Holywood in the south-west; Kilwinning in Ayrshire; Deer in Buchan. Unwanted monastic buildings, the church included, of course fell into ruin or were used as quarries for ready-cut stone, but in our own times the monastic buildings, not merely the church, of Iona and Pluscarden have been restored and put to use.

The Reformation Parliament of 1560 made a theological decision in legalising Protestantism and proscribing Catholicism, but enacted nothing constitutional or practical. The pre-reformation incumbents stayed in office with their revenue intact and under no obligation to serve in the new Kirk. Nor was there any change in the process of appointment to parish benefices; the person appointed was not necessarily a Protestant or even sympathetic to Protestantism or acceptable to the reformers. Very soon a financial arrangement was made whereby a benefice-holder in a parish kept all his income if he served in the Protestant Church but only two thirds of it if he did not.[14] The remaining third was taxed and went to the Crown and/or the Kirk, but it was very inefficiently uplifted and was often remitted. John Knox summed up the arrangement from his point of view in a memorable expression, when he said that two thirds went to the devil and one third was divided between God and the devil.[15]

In the monasteries recruitment of new novices ceased, as did the choir office and public Catholic services. The communities, however, remained in place with each individual dwelling-place and portion intact. The tax of the third did not apply to monastic portions; in fact these were treated like modern tax allowances, being deducted from the total income of the monastery before it was assessed for the tax.[16] There seems to have been no public hostility towards the monks, for they were not attacked either verbally or physically, and that was despite their financial security. They had at times to take legal action to get their portion from their commendator, who was no longer a religious superior, but they apparently always won their case, even after 1560. And even after 1560 they retained their religious and monastic titles too – vicar, prior, religious brother, Dene.[17]

Not until 1566–7 did the successor to a deceased benefice-holder have to be a Protestant and at this point all churchmen, monks and regular canons living in their monasteries included, were invited to serve in the Kirk. And not until 1573 did benefice-holders have to accept the Protestant Confession of Faith or suffer deprivation. The General Assembly of 1573 assumed that most monks and canons regular had by then conformed with the new religion, but it did so in an almost casual way; and whatever the degree of truth in the assumption, they had not been obliged to conform as a condition for retaining their lodging and portion.[18]

The story of what happened after 1560 varied from one monastery to another, with much depending on their recruitment in the 1540s and 1550s. All members of the community at Kelso were dead by the summer of 1580, all at Jedburgh by 1588.[19] All but one at Melrose had died by 1586, but the survivor lived until 1609 and for the last four years of his life is recorded as Dene John Watson, bailie depute of Melrose regality.[20] Not many monks are recorded at Balmerino after 1560; the abbot feued the whole establishment in 1565 because of the age and infirmity of the monks, of whom only two were still alive in 1586. In 1574 at Monymusk the sole survivor, described as a poor aged man, sued for arrears of his portion.[21] Others lived longer. A monk of Crossraguel won a suit for his portion in 1602 and another was still alive in 1607, while at Cambuskenneth Robert McCalay protested in 1607 that his rights as last surviving member of the community were being disregarded.[22] The last survivor is perhaps Stephen Mason of Lindores, who became a minister in the Kirk. In 1614, when he was transferred to a new parish, the parishioners complained at being given an old man! He died in 1618, almost sixty years after the Reformation Parliament.[23]

What is more interesting than physical survival is attitude to the Reformation, and it is important to bear in mind that rights to portion and lodging were not dependent on this. Of three canons of Scone suing for their portions in 1575, one, Thomas Cruikshank, was a Protestant minister. At Culross, of nine surviving monks, five accepted Protestantism while the other four refused to do so. The Protestant commendator tried to withhold the portions of these four but was made to pay them.[24]

The religious sympathies of most monks and canons are not recorded. No monk of Balmerino, Crossraguel or Pluscarden served in the reformed Church,[25] and the Crossraguel community certainly seems to have been Catholic in sympathy. Abbot Quintin Kennedy disputed publicly with John Knox in 1562 and John Maxwell was saying Mass in 1568; between 1585 and 1590 the subprior's will was drawn up in traditional Catholic language, Gilbert Kennedy was in trouble for profaning the sacraments (that is, administering them with Catholic rites) and Adam Maxwell was causing trouble to the ministers.[26] A Newbattle monk was saying Mass in 1567, a monk of Pluscarden was baptising with Catholic rites in the 1590s.[27]

Choir office continued, at least for a time, at Crossraguel, Kilwinning and Sweetheart.[28] Some monks of Dunfermline served in the Protestant Kirk but in 1580 choir office was still being recited, though not in public, and the monks saw to the safe-keeping of St Margaret's relics. Both these and the relics of St Ninian at Whithorn were taken abroad for safety.[29] In 1562 the monks of Melrose had apparently elected one of their own number as abbot and he travelled to Cîteaux to ask the general chapter for help.[30] Six monks of the charterhouse went abroad to continue their eremitical life, while two became Protestants in Perth.[31] Five men in the Borders – three canons of Dryburgh, a monk of Coldingham and one from Melrose – were in trouble in 1569 for exercising their priestly functions.[32] The situation after 1560 was anything but cut and dried.

Two episodes were of larger significance. In 1563 there was a concerted but short-lived effort to restore Catholicism in the west and south-west, with monks of Crossraguel and Paisley and canons of Whithorn deeply involved.[33] Also in the south-west Gilbert Brown, a young monk recorded at Sweetheart shortly before 1560, went to St Andrews university in the early 1560s and conformed with Protestantism for a time. He was made commendator of Sweetheart in 1565, became a vigorous Catholic and in 1587 was ordained priest at Paris. For three decades he almost single-handedly kept Catholicism alive in the south-west.[34]

A Protestant minister's role was to preach and administer the sacraments. In the period immediately after 1560, because there were not enough ministers to go round, men were recruited as a temporary measure to read a service on Sundays. These readers were of limited value, they were not employed full-time and did not receive a full salary. (Exhorters, an intermediate category who preached as well as reading the service, existed for about ten years but are here included under readers.) The General Assembly of 1573, believing (perhaps rightly) that most surviving canons, monks and friars had 'made profession of the true religion', wanted them to serve as readers where appointed.[35]

In fact, far more monks and canons served in the Kirk than upheld Catholicism. The prime example is St Andrews, and it is striking that it was the monasteries where observance was good and recruitment continued well that helped the reformed Church the most. Nine men entered at St Andrews in the 1550s, and after 1560 the priory made a notable contribution to the ministry of the reformed Church. The subprior John Winram became Protestant superintendent of Fife (roughly the equivalent of a bishop), fifteen or sixteen canons served as ministers and five as readers, while St Leonard's became a Protestant college and the Augustinian monastic chapter continued as the chapter of the Protestant bishopric.[36]

The next most valuable monastery for the reformed Kirk was Lindores, which supplied four ministers and five readers (see map section).[37] One of the ministers was short-lived, or at least his ministerial career was. The other three, typically, were mobile. Stephen Mason served in Aberdeenshire from 1563, the other two served first in Fife – Andrew Forester being minister at Dysart and Wemyss, Patrick Galt at Portmoak and Kinglassie, then at Abdie and Abernethy. Both then moved much further away. The readers, on the other hand, retained their quarters and subsistence in the monastery and merely officiated on Sundays in the neighbourhood. Between them in the 1560s they served at Abdie, Dunbog, Flisk, Creich, Monimail, Collessie, Auchtermuchty and Strathmiglo; and in the 1570s another ex-monk served at Moonzie. Monks of Lindores between them provided Protestant worship at all the parish churches in the vicinity of their monastery.

Arbroath came next with four ministers and one reader, followed by Holyrood with three ministers and possibly a reader. Quite often it cannot be said for certain that a minister or reader and a monk with the same name were the same person. One has to go on probabilities, for instance if the name was uncommon or the parish was near the monastery or appropriated to it. Thus Deer provided two, perhaps three, ministers; Scone provided two ministers and two readers. All these monasteries, except perhaps Deer, had recruits in the years before 1560. Nine other monasteries supplied one minister each. The minister at Kilwinning, William Kirkpatrick, used the abbey church as his kirk, and his monastic quarters as the manse for himself and his wife.[38] Dunfermline provided the celebrated John Durie, who succeeded John Knox as minister at St Giles' in Edinburgh, and also four readers. At Kinloss Abbot Walter Reid financed John Philip, the minister from the community, when the Kirk was unable to do so, and also supported a minister in an appropriated church.[39]

Other monasteries, particularly those of canons, provided readers rather than ministers. Dryburgh supplied three as well as a minister; from Cambuskenneth and Inchaffray came three, and from Inchcolm two or perhaps three. Three Premonstratensian houses in the south-west, Whithorn, Tongland and Holywood, provided no less than seventeen readers. The six from Whithorn all served in churches very near the priory (see map section) and surely continued to make use of their monastic portion and lodging. The total contribution of the monasteries was forty ministers and fifty-one readers, though it is perhaps more illuminating to look at the regions where they served. In Dumfries and Galloway half the readers came from the monasteries, providing the reformed Church with widespread though limited help at a crucial time of need.[40] In the east (Edinburgh, Fife and north of Tay) were a superintendent, over thirty ministers and over twenty readers. The monasteries, especially St Andrews, played a very important role in the success of the Reformation in the eastern Lowlands.

It has usually been said that a man became a reader if he lacked the education to be a minister. There is no evidence that this is true of monk-readers and in some cases it is manifestly false. For instance the Lindores monk-reader, Robert Williamson, was a notary, and it was Dunfermline Abbey's one minister, not any of its four readers, whose literacy was criticised. It seems far more likely that readers were simply less committed to the reformed Church than ministers. Perhaps they thought it better to supply a Protestant service than to leave the people without any. And even if they were Protestant by conviction, they were not willing to undertake the labours of full-time ministry or leave their monastic quarters. Some in fact were simply readers in their own monastic church.

Whereas these cases show merely a lack of evidence of commitment to Protestantism, in three others there is positive evidence of a lack of such commitment, or at the very least of uncertainty. Robert Milne (Dryburgh) before he was a reader, William Telfer (Whithorn) while he was a reader, and John Logan (Sweetheart) after he had ceased to be a reader, were in trouble for saying Mass.[41] There was some, not very much, financial inducement for a monk or canon already enjoying a portion to be a reader, though a vicarage which sometimes went with it was far more attractive. Some men hesitated or changed their mind, as one would expect in a revolution. Gilbert Brown for instance, the Catholic champion already mentioned, had conformed with Protestantism for a time.[42] A Holyrood canon-vicar, John Wilson, having embraced Protestantism in 1560, was later in trouble for saying Mass.[43]

Of the pre-reformation monastic vicars, not one became a minister, though some did become readers.[44] If they did not serve in the reformed Church, they were required to give up one third of their income. Some did this, some did not, some were actually so badly in arrears that they incurred the legal penalty of horning (being declared outlaw),[45] but unwillingness to pay taxes is no safe indication of a person's religious convictions. In the 1570s, however, Stephen Moffat (Holyrood) and John Chatto (Dryburgh) were deprived of their vicarages because they refused to accept the Protestant Confession of Faith.[46]

Monasteries helped the Reformation in an area perhaps even more important than the ministry. Since Protestant church services were purged of all the Catholic trappings, all the ceremonial and music and all the variations of the liturgical year, the only addition to the bald spoken word was the music of the vernacular psalter. This most important feature was provided by the musical expertise of pre-reformation monks and canons. The driving force behind the new Scottish Psalter was Thomas Wood, monk of Lindores, with three other men composing the melodies. These were John Angus, monk of Dunfermline, David Peebles, canon of St Andrews, and Andrew Blackhall, canon of Holyrood and a minister.[47] It is a striking example of pre-reformation vitality serving the post-reformation Church.

It is a supremely important fact that before 1560 no layman could be a commendator in Scotland. Monastic vows and major orders were equally a bar to valid marriage, and therefore no abbot or commendator could have a legitimate child.[48] The best he could do was to resign in favour of a nephew, and of course monastic property could be feued to one's kin. In any case, even though powerful local families did corner abbacies and bailieships, and great churchmen did acquire commends of abbeys, the nature of a monastic prelacy was such that it could not become hereditary. Provision by Rome was needed for each succeeding prelate.

After 1560 the Crown assumed the power of provision previously exercised by Rome, which simply meant that a Crown grant was needed instead of Roman provision. The nature of a monastic prelacy did not change: it was still not hereditary.[49] Although a commendator could now have a legitimate son, that son could not be heir to his father's monastic office – a fresh grant of the commend was needed. In the only case of a legitimate son being born to a commendator before 1560, that of Mark Ker at Newbattle (and only because Ker took extraordinary measures to retain his abbacy after contracting marriage), the son needed a fresh grant of Newbattle.[50]

The Crown considered that it had rights over monastic property. In 1587 the monasteries and their lands were annexed to the Crown, and then or later the lands of most monasteries were erected into hereditary temporal lordships.[51] It is usually said that the families of pre-reformation abbots or commendators were the greatest beneficiaries. In point of fact they acquired the lands feued to them, but not many acquired the lordship. In fifteen monasteries at least, the prelacy had passed before 1560 to a member of the same family:[52]

Kinloss: Robert and Walter Reid
Crossraguel: William and Quintin Kennedy
Arbroath, Dunfermline, Melrose: various Beatons or Duries (sister's sons)[53]
Culross: Colvilles
Paisley: Hamiltons (and earlier, Shaws)[54]
Jedburgh: Humes
Kelso: Kers
Coldingham: Humes, then Blackadders[55]
Dryburgh (with Inchmahome): Erskines
St Andrews: John and Patrick Hepburn
Deer: Keiths, Earls Marischal

Whithorn: Flemings[56]

Pittenweem: Formans and John Rule (nephew)[57]

Of these fifteen prelacies, only five were retained by the associated families: Colvilles remained at Culross, Hamiltons at Paisley, Humes at Jedburgh, Erskines at Dryburgh, Earls Marischal at Deer. At Melrose, Kelso, Coldingham and St Andrews the appointment of an illegitimate infant son of James V had broken the grip, or at least the succession, of a family.[58] Although Kelso and Coldingham went eventually to Kers and Humes respectively, this was clearly due to their local standing in later decades rather than to any hold acquired before 1560.

Three families retained an abbacy more recently acquired: Mark Ker's son at Newbattle, Stewarts at Inchcolm, Hamiltons at Arbroath. One monastery went to the hereditary bailie: Kilwinning to the Earl of Eglinton. The two cathedral priories and the two monasteries annexed to bishoprics (Tongland, Iona) went to the Protestant bishoprics. Thus, even if most monastic lands were bestowed on temporal lords, only a fraction of these were of the same family as the pre-reformation abbots or commendators. The reformed Church got none of the land feued before 1560 and was not a major beneficiary of the post-reformation settlement of monastic property. Just as a footnote, one can add that a canon of Inchaffray, Patrick Murray, a vicar and a reader in the Kirk, managed to found a landed family with church revenues.[59]

The disposal of monastic lands and revenues, however, was not the end of the story. One of the strangest episodes in all monastic history now provided an unexpected sequel.[60] Celtic monks from the sixth century on had taken Christianity and monasticism to widespread regions of the Continent. By the end of the eleventh century their activity was confined to the south German-speaking lands and they had accepted the Rule of St Benedict. They founded ten Benedictine monasteries, centred on the abbey of St James in Ratisbon (Regensburg on the Danube). Though these were in Germany, all the monks were Celts, Gaelic speakers from Ireland (and perhaps also present-day Scotland).

These foundations were known as the monasteries of the Scots, the *monasteria Scotorum* or *Schottenklöster*. Originally the terms 'Scot' and 'Scotland' referred to what is the present-day Ireland, but their meaning changed and they came to denote present-day Scotland.

The Irish monks in Germany, however, continued to use the old name. The story therefore arose, and was widely believed in Scotland and Germany, that the foundations had originally been made by Scots from Scotland and wrongfully taken from them by Irish monks.

In the fifteenth century the fortunes of these Irish monasteries declined as recruitment from Ireland withered away. Then came the fateful *coup*. There was in Ratisbon a large colony of Scots traders and in 1515 monks from Scotland, no doubt helped by these influential resident Scots, took over the surviving Irish houses, convinced that they were theirs by right. John Denys, a monk of Newbattle, became prior in Ratisbon. In 1578 Ninian Winzet, formerly schoolmaster in Linlithgow and a vigorous opponent of John Knox, was provided as abbot of Ratisbon and was joined by John Hamilton, monk of Paisley. The three *Schottenklöster* that survived into the seventeenth century became counter-reformation centres, recruiting from Scotland, sending missionary priests to Scotland and taking part in Jacobite activities. They also contributed greatly to German cultural life and scientific development. In 1862, when the last surviving Scottish monastery on German soil finally came to an end, the last monk in Ratisbon, Father Anselm Robertson from Fochabers, returned to Scotland and assisted in founding the monastery at Fort Augustus. A slender but unbroken thread links pre-reformation and present-day monastic life in Scotland.

## NOTES

1. Herkless and Hannay, *St Leonard*; *St A. Acta*, pp. lx–lxii; Durkan, 'Cultural Background', pp. 293–5; A. F. S. Pearson, 'Alesius and the English Reformation', RSCHS, x (1949), pp. 57–87; Dilworth, 'Canons', 164–6. See p. 35 above.
2. Dilworth, 'Canons', 166–8; Durkan, 'Evangelicals', pp. 134–7, 148–9; J. Durkan, 'Heresy in Scotland: the second phase, 1546–58', RSCHS, 24 (1992), p. 342.
3. J. K. Hewison, 'Sir John Macbrair', TDGAS, 3rd Ser. ix (1924), pp. 158–68; Durkan, 'Local Heretics', pp. 74–7; Durkan, 'Heresy in Scotland', pp. 328–9, 340; D. Calderwood, *The History of the Kirk of Scotland* (Wodrow Society, 1842), i, pp. 113–14; Verschuur, 'Perth Charterhouse', p. 3.
4. Durkan, 'Local Heretics', p. 71; Dilworth, 'Canons', 168–9.
5. Durkan, 'Paisley', pp. 121–2.
6. McRoberts, *Essays*, p. 56; A. E. Jones, *The Trial of Joan of Arc* (Chichester, 1980), pp. 29ff.
7. *CSP Scot.*, i passim.

8. McRoberts, *St Andrews*, p. 119; McRoberts, 'Material Destruction', p. 431; *CSP Scot.*, i, p. 212; *C. A. Chrs*, ii, pp. 278–9.
9. Knox, *History*, i, p. 213; *Cambusk. Reg.*, pp. cvii–cviii.
10. Ross, 'Religious Houses', p. 213; McRoberts, 'Material Destruction', pp. 429–40; Knox, *History*, i, pp. 162–3.
11. Verschuur, 'Perth Charterhouse', pp. 8–9.
12. A. R. Anderson, 'Scottish Medieval Churches still used for Divine Service', *TSES*, xii (1939), pp. 111–16; McRoberts, 'Material Destruction', pp. 447–51.
13. Dilworth, *Scots in Franconia*, pp. 200–1.
14. Donaldson, 'Parish Clergy', pp. 131–4; *RSS*, v, pp. ii–xiii; G. Donaldson, *The Scottish Reformation* (Cambridge, 1960), pp. 67–75.
15. *Thirds of Benefices*, passim; Knox, *History*, i, p. lix.
16. Donaldson, 'Parish Clergy', pp. 136–7; *Thirds of Benefices*, p. xiv; Macphail, *Pluscardyn*, pp. 255–6.
17. Donaldson, 'Galloway Clergy', p. 46; *Wigt. Chrs*, p. 56; Donaldson, 'Parish Clergy', pp. 132–3. See nn. 20, 22.
18. Donaldson, 'Parish Clergy', pp. 143–4; *BUK*, i, p. 280.
19. *RSS*, viii, no. 1374; Dilworth, 'Border Abbeys', p. 236.
20. Dilworth, 'Monks and Ministers', p. 203; *Melrose Recs*, i, pp. 3–82.
21. SRO, RH 6/1990; *APS*, iv, pp. 431–3; *RPC*, ii, pp. 389–90.
22. Fergusson, 'Last Monks', pp. 59–60; *NLS*, Chr. 4035.
23. Dilworth, 'Monks and Ministers', p. 213.
24. *RSS*, vii, no. 272; Haws, *Parish Clergy*, p. 172; Douglas, 'Culross', p. 93.
25. Antecedents of Protestant clergy are in Haws, *Parish Clergy*, pp. 250–323.
26. Ross, 'Religious Orders', pp. 229–31; *BUK*, ii, p. 722; *RPC*, iv, p. 522.
27. J. Durkan, 'William Murdoch and the Early Jesuit Mission in Scotland', *IR*, 35 (1984), p. 4; M. H. B. Sanderson, 'Catholic Recusancy in Scotland in the Sixteenth Century', *IR*, 21 (1970), p. 103.
28. Cowan, 'Monastic Ideal', p. 43; *BUK*, i, p. 6.
29. Dilworth, 'Monks and Ministers', p. 216; McRoberts, 'Material Destruction', p. 443n; McRoberts, *St Margaret*, pp. 29–33; Brooke, *St Ninian*, p. 4.
30. Canivez, *Statuta*, 1562, no. 47.
31. Hogg, 'Perth Charterhouse', pp. 168–9; Dilworth, 'Monks and Ministers', pp. 205–6.
32. *RPC*, ii, p. 40.
33. *Criminal Trials in Scotland from 1488 to 1624*, ed. R. Pitcairn (Bannatyne and Maitland Clubs, 1833), i, pp. 427–8*; *A Diurnal of Remarkable Occurrents … till the year 1575* (Bannatyne and Maitland Club, 1833), pp. 75–6.
34. Dilworth, 'Gilbert Brown', pp. 153–6.
35. *BUK*, i, p. 280; *Thirds of Benefices*, p. xxiin.
36. Dilworth, 'Augustinian Chapter', pp. 26–30; 'Canons', 171–2.
37. The evidence for recruitment in each house and service in the Protestant Church is found in Haws, *Parish Clergy*, pp. 250–323 and Dilworth's articles: 'Monks and Ministers' for Lindores, Arbroath, Kilwinning and Dunfermline; 'Canons' for Holyrood, Scone and other houses of canons regular; 'Border Abbeys' for Dryburgh. Other references are supplementary.
38. See also Sanderson, 'Kilwinning', pp. 113–22.
39. *RPC*, i, pp. 680–1, 684; *Kinloss Recs*, pp. 159–60.

40. Donaldson, 'Galloway Clergy', pp. 43–59.
41. Haws, *Parish Clergy*, pp. 45, 54, 165, 178; Ross, 'Religious Orders', p. 230.
42. Dilworth, 'Gilbert Brown', p. 153.
43. *The Register of the Kirk-Session of St Andrews*, ed. D. H. Fleming (SHS 1889), i, pp. 11–13, 193; Haws, *Parish Clergy*, p. 137.
44. Haws, *Parish Clergy* passim.
45. *Thirds of Benefices* passim.
46. Haws, *Parish Clergy*, pp. 197, 238.
47. N. Livingston, *The Scottish Metrical Psalter of A.D. 1635* (Glasgow, 1864), p. 48; Laing, 'Scottish Psalter', pp. 445–58; K. Elliott, 'Scottish Music of the Early Reformed Church', *TSES*, xv pt. 2 (1961), pp. 18–32.
48. Dilworth, 'Commendator System', pp. 58–9.
49. *RSS*, v, pp. ii–vii; *RPC*, 2nd Ser., i, p. cxxxv.
50. *MRHS*, p. 77; Dilworth, 'Commendator System', pp. 60–1, 62; Sanderson, *Mary Stewart's People*, p. 177.
51. For each house see *MRHS* passim; *RPC*, 2nd Ser., i, pp. cxxxii–cxxxv, cxliv–cxlvi.
52. *MRHS* passim. Further references give supplementary data.
53. For the Beaton–Durie relationship and monastic hegemony see *DSCHT*, pp. 65, 66, 266; Dowden, *Bishops*, p. 374.
54. Lees, *Paisley*, pp. 137–45.
55. Dilworth, 'Coldingham', pp. 118–26.
56. Dilworth, *Whithorn*, pp. 5–7.
57. Dilworth, 'Dependent Priories', p. 58.
58. Dilworth, 'Commendator System', pp. 60, 64.
59. Dilworth, 'Canons', 176–7.
60. *MRHS*, pp. 240–4; Dilworth, *Scots in Franconia*, pp. 11–30, 267–9; *DSCHT*, p. 746.

# Abbreviations

The abbreviations for source material are taken almost entirely from the recommended list in the supplement to *The Scottish Historical Review* of October 1963. Others follow the same principles. A few titles have been abbreviated in the source references, though there was no advantage in doing so, in order to include them in the following list and so increase its value as a bibliography.

*A. B. Ill.*: *Illustrations of the Topography and Antiquities of the Shires of Aberdeen and Banff* (Spalding Club, 1847–69).

*ACSB*: *The Apostolic Camera and Scottish Benefices 1418–88*, ed. A. I. Cameron (Oxford, 1934).

*ADCP*: *Acts of the Lords of Council in Public Affairs 1501–1554*, ed. R. K. Hannay (Edinburgh, 1932).

*AHCAG*: *Archeological and Historical Collections relating to Ayrshire and Galloway* (1878–99).

*APS*: *The Acts of the Parliaments of Scotland*, ed. T. Thomson and C. Innes (Edinburgh, 1814–75).

*Arbroath Lib.*: *Liber S. Thome de Aberbrothoc* (Bannatyne Club, 1848–56).

Backmund, *Monasticon*: N. Backmund, *Monasticon Praemonstratense* (Straubing, 1949–56).

Backmund, 'Premonstratensian Order': N. Backmund, 'The Premonstratensian Order in Scotland', *IR*, iv (1953), pp. 25–41.

Barrow, *Kingdom of Scots*: G. W. S. Barrow, *The Kingdom of the Scots* (London, 1973).

*Beauly Chrs*: *The Charters of the Priory of Beauly* (Grampian Club, 1877).

Beckett, 'Perth Charterhouse': W. N. M. Beckett, 'The Perth Charterhouse before 1500', *Analecta Cartusiana*, 128 (1988), pp. 1–74.

Brady, *Episcopal Succession*: W. M. Brady, *The Episcopal Succession in England, Scotland and Ireland 1400–1875* (Rome, 1876–7).

Brooke, *St Ninian*: D. Brooke, *The Medieval Cult of Saint Ninian* (Whithorn, 1987).

BUK: *Acts and Proceedings of the General Assemblies (Booke of the Universall Kirk)*, (Bannatyne and Maitland Clubs, 1839–45).

CAAS: *Collections of the Ayrshire Archaeological and Natural History Society* (1947–).

*C. A. Chrs:* *Charters of the Abbey of Coupar Angus*, ed. D. E. Easson (SHS, 1947).

*C. A. Rent.:* *Rental Book of the Cistercian Abbey of Cupar Angus* (Grampian Club, 1879–80).

*Cambusk. Reg.:* *Registrum Monasterii S. Marie de Cambuskenneth* (Grampian Club, 1872).

Canivez, *Statuta:* J. M. Canivez, *Statuta Capitulorum Generalium Ordinis Cisterciensis 1116–1786* (Louvain, 1933–41).

Colvin, *White Canons:* H. M. Colvin, *The White Canons in England* (Oxford, 1951).

Coulton, *Scottish Abbeys:* G. G. Coulton, *Scottish Abbeys and Social Life* (Cambridge, 1933).

Cousin, *Précis:* P. Cousin, *Précis d'Histoire Monastique* (Paris, 1956).

Cowan, 'Appropriation': I. B. Cowan, 'Some Aspects of the Appropriation of Parish Churches in Medieval Scotland', *RSCHS*, 13 (1959), pp. 203–22.

Cowan, 'Ayrshire Abbeys': I. B. Cowan, 'Ayrshire Abbeys: Crossraguel and Kilwinning', *CAAS*, xiv, no. 7 (1986), pp. 265–95.

Cowan, 'Cure of Souls': I. B. Cowan, 'The Religious and the Cure of Souls in Medieval Scotland', *RSCHS*, xiv (1962), pp. 215–29.

Cowan, 'Monastic Ideal': 'The Monastic Ideal' in I. B. Cowan, *The Scottish Reformation* (London, 1982), pp. 27–48.

Cowan, *Parishes:* I. B. Cowan, *The Parishes of Medieval Scotland* (SRS, 1967).

CPL: *Calendar of Entries in the Papal Registers relating to Great Britain and Ireland: Papal Letters*, ed. W. H. Bliss and others (London, 1893–).

*Crossraguel Chrs:* *Charters of the Abbey of Crossraguel* (AHCAG, 1886).

Cruden, *Medieval Churches:* S. Cruden, *Scottish Medieval Churches* (Edinburgh, 1986).

CSP *Scot.:* *Calendar of the State Papers relating to Scotland … 1547–1603*, ed. J. Bain and others (Edinburgh, 1898–).

CSSR: *Calendar of Scottish Supplications to Rome*, i–iii (SHS 1934, 1956, 1970), iv (Glasgow, 1983).

DHGE: *Dictionnaire d'Histoire et Géographie Ecclésiastiques* (1912–).

Dickinson, *Origins:* J. C. Dickinson, *The Origins of the Austin Canons* (London, 1950).

Dilworth, 'Augustinian Chapter': M. Dilworth, 'The Augustinian Chapter of St Andrews', *IR*, 25 (1974), pp. 15–30.

Dilworth, 'Border Abbeys': M. Dilworth, 'The Border Abbeys in the Sixteenth Century', *RSCHS*, xxi (1983), pp. 233–47.

Dilworth, 'Canons': M. Dilworth, 'Canons Regular and the Reformation', in *The Renaissance in Scotland*, ed. A. A. MacDonald and M. Lynch (1994), 164–82.

Dilworth, 'Coldingham': M. Dilworth, 'Coldingham Priory and the Reformation', *IR*, 23 (1972), pp. 115–37.

Dilworth, 'Commendator System': M. Dilworth, 'The Commendator System in Scotland', IR, 37 (1986), pp. 51–72.
Dilworth, 'Dependent Priories': M. Dilworth, 'The Dependent Priories of St Andrews', IR, 26 (1975), pp. 56–64.
Dilworth, 'Franco-Scottish Efforts': M. Dilworth, 'Franco-Scottish Efforts at Monastic Reform 1500–1560', RSCHS, 25 (1994, forthcoming).
Dilworth, 'Gilbert Brown': M. Dilworth, 'Abbot Gilbert Brown: A Sketch of his Career', IR, 40 (1989), pp. 153–8.
Dilworth, 'Iona': M. Dilworth, 'Iona Abbey and the Reformation', *Scottish Gaelic Studies*, xii pt 1 (1971), pp. 77–109.
Dilworth, 'Literacy': M. Dilworth, 'Literacy of Pre-Reformation Monks', IR, 24 (1973), pp. 71–2.
Dilworth, 'Monks and Ministers': M. Dilworth, 'Monks and Ministers after 1560', RSCHS, 18 (1974), pp. 201–21.
Dilworth, *Scots in Franconia*: *The Scots in Franconia: A Century of Monastic Life* (Edinburgh, 1974).
Dilworth, 'Social Origins': M. Dilworth, 'The Social Origins of Scottish Medieval Monks', RSCHS, xx (1980), pp. 197–209.
Dilworth, *Whithorn*: M. Dilworth, *Whithorn Priory in the Late Middle Ages* (Whithorn, 1994).
Donaldson, 'Galloway Clergy': G. Donaldson, 'The Galloway Clergy at the Reformation', TDGAS, 3rd Ser. 30 (1953), pp. 42–59.
Donaldson, 'Parish Clergy': G. Donaldson, 'The Parish Clergy and the Reformation', in McRoberts, *Essays*, pp. 129–44.
Douglas, 'Culross': W. Douglas, 'Culross Abbey and its Charters', PSAS, 60 (1927), pp. 67–94.
Dowden, *Bishops*: J. Dowden, *The Bishops of Scotland* (Glasgow, 1912).
Dowden, *Medieval Church*: J. Dowden, *The Medieval Church in Scotland* (Glasgow, 1910).
DSCHT: *Dictionary of Scottish Church History and Theology* (Edinburgh, 1993).
Dunbar, *Scot Kings*: A. H. Dunbar, *Scottish Kings: A Revised Chronology of Scottish History 1005–1625* (2nd edn Edinburgh, 1906).
*Dunfermline Ct. Bk*: *Regality of Dunfermline Court Book 1531–1538*, ed. J. M. Webster and A. A. M. Duncan (Dunfermline, 1953).
*Dunfermline Reg.*: *Registrum de Dunfermelyn* (Bannatyne Club, 1842).
Durkan, 'Care of Poor': J. Durkan, 'Care of the Poor: Pre-Reformation Hospitals', in McRoberts, *Essays*, pp. 116–28.
Durkan, 'Cultural Background': J. Durkan, 'The Cultural Background in Sixteenth-Century Scotland', in McRoberts, *Essays*, pp. 274–331.
Durkan, 'Education': J. Durkan, 'Education in the Century of the Reformation', in McRoberts, *Essays*, pp. 145–68.
Durkan, 'Evangelicals': J. Durkan, 'Scottish "Evangelicals" in the Patronage of Thomas Cromwell', RSCHS, 21 pt 2 (1982), pp. 127–56.
Durkan, 'Law Chronicle': J. Durkan, 'St Andrews in the John Law Chronicle', IR, 25 (1974), pp. 49–62.
Durkan, 'Local Heretics': J. Durkan, 'Some Local Heretics', TDGAS, 3rd Ser. 36 (1957–8), pp. 67–77.

Durkan, 'Paisley': J. Durkan, 'Paisley Abbey in the Sixteenth Century', *IR*, 27 (1976), pp. 110–26.
Easson, 'Education': D. E. Easson, 'The Medieval Church in Scotland and Education', *RSCHS*, vi (1938), pp. 13–26.
Easson, 'Reformation': D. E. Easson, 'The Reformation and the Monasteries in Scotland and England: Some Comparisons', *TSES*, xv pt 1 (1957), pp. 7–23.
*ESL:* J. Durkan and A. Ross, *Early Scottish Libraries* (Glasgow, 1961).
Fergusson, 'Last Monks': 'The Last Monks of Crossraguel', in J. Fergusson, *The White Hind* (London, 1963), pp. 54–66.
Ferrerius, *Historia:* *Ferrerii Historia Abbatum de Kynlos* (Bannatyne Club, 1839). Pp. 36–53, 55–86 are reprinted in *Kinloss Recs*, pp. 46–63, 16–46.
Finnie, 'House of Hamilton': E. Finnie, 'The House of Hamilton', *IR*, 36 (1985), pp. 3–28.
Fleming, *Reformation:* D. H. Fleming, *The Reformation in Scotland* (London, 1910).
Forbes, *Kalendars:* A. P. Forbes, *Kalendars of Scottish Saints* (Edinburgh, 1872).
Hannay, 'Papal Bulls': R. K. Hannay, 'Some Papal Bulls among the Hamilton Papers', *SHR*, 22 (1925), pp. 25–41.
Haws, *Parish Clergy:* C. H. Haws, *Scottish Parish Clergy at the Reformation 1540–1574* (*SRS*, 1972).
Henry, 'Glenluce': D. Henry, 'Glenluce Abbey', *AHCAG*, v (1885), pp. 125–88.
Herkless and Hannay, *Archbishops:* J. Herkless and R. K. Hannay, *The Archbishops of St Andrews* (Edinburgh, 1907–15).
Herkless and Hannay, *St Leonard:* J. Herkless and R. K. Hannay, *The College of St Leonard* (Edinburgh, 1905).
Hogg, 'Perth Charterhouse': A. Hogg, 'Sidelights on the Perth Charterhouse', *IR*, xix (1968), pp. 168–9.
*IR:* *The Innes Review* (1950–).
*James IV Letters:* *The Letters of James the Fourth 1505–13*, ed. R. K. Hannay and R. L. Mackie (*SHS*, 1953).
*James V Letters:* *The Letters of James V*, ed. R. K. Hannay and D. Hay (Edinburgh, 1954).
*Kelso Lib.:* *Liber S. Marie de Calchou* (Bannatyne Club, 1846).
Ker, *Kilwinning:* W. L. Ker, *Kilwinning Abbey* (Ardrossan, ND).
Ker, *Medieval Libraries:* N. R. Ker, *Medieval Libraries of Great Britain* (2nd edn London, 1964).
'Kilwinning Collections': 'Collections towards a History of the Monastery of Kilwinning', *AHCAG*, i (1878), pp. 115–222.
*Kinloss Recs:* *Records of the Monastery of Kinloss*, ed. J. Stuart (Edinburgh, 1872).
*Kirkintilloch Ct. Bk:* *Court Book of the Burgh of Kirkintilloch 1658–1694*, ed. G. S. Pryde (SHS, 1963).
Knowles, *Christian Monasticism:* D. Knowles, *Christian Monasticism* (London, 1969).

Knowles, *Monastic Order:* D. Knowles, *The Monastic Order in England* (Cambridge, 1940).
Knowles, *Religious Orders:* D. Knowles, *The Religious Orders in England* (Cambridge, 1948–59).
Knox, *History:* *John Knox's History of the Reformation*, ed. W. C. Dickinson (Edinburgh, 1949).
*Laing Chrs:* *Calendar of the Laing Charters 854–1837*, ed. J. Anderson (Edinburgh, 1899).
Laing, 'Scottish Psalter': D. Laing, 'An Account of the Scottish Psalter of A.D. 1566', PSAS, vii (1870), pp. 445–58.
Lees, *Paisley:* J. C. Lees, *The Abbey of Paisley* (Paisley, 1878).
Lynch, *Scotland:* M. Lynch, *Scotland: A New History* (London, 1991).
Macphail, *Pluscardyn:* S. R. Macphail, *The Religious House of Pluscardyn* (Edinburgh, 1881).
Malden, *Paisley:* J. Malden, *The Abbey and Monastery of Paisley* (Renfrew, 1993).
McKay, 'Heid Pilgrimages': D. McKay, 'The Four Heid Pilgrimages of Scotland', *IR*, xix (1968), pp. 76–7.
McRoberts, 'Culross': D. McRoberts, 'Culross in the Diocese of Dunblane', *The Society of Friends of Dunblane Cathedral*, x pt 4 (1969), pp. 91-8.
McRoberts, *Essays:* *Essays on the Scottish Reformation 1513–1625*, ed. D. McRoberts (Glasgow, 1962).
McRoberts, 'Material Destruction': D. McRoberts, 'Material Destruction Caused by the Scottish Reformation', in McRoberts, *Essays*, pp. 415–62.
McRoberts, *St Andrews:* *The Medieval Church of St Andrews*, ed. D. McRoberts (Glasgow, 1976).
McRoberts, *St Margaret:* D. McRoberts, *St Margaret: Queen of Scotland* (Glasgow, ND).
*Melrose Recs:* *Selections from the Records of the Regality of Melrose* (SHS, 1914–17).
Morton, *Monastic Annals:* J. Morton, *The Monastic Annals of Teviotdale* (Edinburgh, 1832).
*MRHS:* I. B. Cowan and D. E. Easson, *Medieval Religious Houses: Scotland* (2nd edn London, 1976).
*Newbattle Reg.:* *Registrum S. Marie de Neubotle* (Bannatyne Club, 1849).
Nicholson, *Scotland:* R. Nicholson, *Scotland: The Later Middle Ages* (Edinburgh, 1974).
NLS: National Library of Scotland.
Patrick, *Statutes:* *Statutes of the Scottish Church*, ed D. Patrick (SHS, 1907).
*PSAS:* *Proceedings of the Society of Antiquaries of Scotland* (1851–).
Reid, 'Clerical Taxation': W. S. Reid, 'Clerical Taxation: The Scottish Alternative to Dissolution of the Monasteries, 1530–1560', *Catholic Historical Review*, 35 (1948), pp. 129–53.

Richardinus, *Commentary:* *Commentary on the Rule of St Augustine by Robertus Richardinus*, ed. G. G. Coulton (SHS, 1935).

*RMS:* *Registrum Magni Sigilli Regum Scotorum*, ed. J. M. Thomson and others (Edinburgh, 1882–1914).

Ross, 'Religious Orders': A. Ross, 'Some Notes on the Religious Orders in Pre-Reformation Scotland', in McRoberts, *Essays*, pp. 185–244.

*RPC:* *The Register of the Privy Council of Scotland*, ed. J. H. Burton and others (Edinburgh, 1877–).

*RSCHS:* *Records of the Scottish Church History Society* (1923–).

*RSS:* *Registrum Secreti Sigilli Regum Scotorum*, ed. J. M. Thomson and others (Edinburgh, 1908–).

Sanderson, 'Aspects': M. H. B. Sanderson, 'Some Aspects of the Church in Scottish Society in the Era of the Reformation', *RSCHS*, 17 (1971), pp. 81–98.

Sanderson, 'Feuars': M. H. B. Sanderson, 'The Feuars of Kirklands', *SHR*, 52 (1973), pp. 117–36.

Sanderson, 'Kilwinning': M. H. B. Sanderson, 'Kilwinning at the Time of the Reformation', *CAAS*, (1972), pp. 101–29.

Sanderson, 'Kirkmen': M. H. B. Sanderson, 'Kirkmen and their Tenants in the Era of the Reformation', *RSCHS*, 18 (1974), pp. 26–42.

Sanderson, 'Manse and Glebe': M. H. B. Sanderson, 'Manse and Glebe in the Sixteenth Century', *RSCHS*, xix pt 1 (1975), pp. 81–92.

Sanderson, *Mary Stewart's People:* M. H. B. Sanderson, *Mary Stewart's People* (Edinburgh, 1987).

Sanderson, 'Mauchline': M. H. B. Sanderson, 'Mauchline Account Books of Melrose 1527–28', *CAAS*, xi pt 5 (1975), pp. 85–107.

Sanderson, *Rural Society:* M. H. B. Sanderson, *Scottish Rural Society in the Sixteenth Century* (Edinburgh, 1982).

Schmitz, *Histoire:* P. Schmitz, *Histoire de l'Ordre de Saint-Benoît* (Maredsous, 1948–56).

*Scone Lib.:* *Liber Ecclesie de Scon* (Bannatyne and Maitland Clubs, 1843).

*Scots Peerage:* *The Scot's Peerage*, ed. J. B. Paul (Edinburgh, 1910–14).

*SHR:* *The Scottish Historical Review* (1903–28, 1947–).

SHS: Scottish History Society.

*Source Book:* *A Source Book of Scottish History*, ii, ed. W. C. Dickinson and others (2nd edn Edinburgh, 1958).

SRO: Scottish Record Office.

SRS: Scottish Record Society.

*St A. Acta:* *Acta Facultatis Artium Universitatis Sanctiandree 1413–1588*, ed. A. I. Dunlop (SHS, 1964).

*St A. Cop.:* *Copiale Prioratus Sanctiandree*, ed. J. H. Baxter (Oxford, 1930).

*St A. Form.:* *St Andrews Formulare 1514–46*, ed. G. Donaldson and C. Macrae (Stair Society, 1942–4).

*St A. Recs:* *Early Records of the University of St Andrews*, ed. J. M. Anderson (SHS, 1926).

STS: Scottish Text Society.

*TA:* *Accounts of the Lord High Treasurer of Scotland*, ed. T. Dickson and J. B. Paul (Edinburgh, 1877–1916).

Talbot, *Letters:* *Letters from the English Abbots to the Chapter at Cîteaux*, ed. C. H. Talbot (London, 1967).
TDGAS: *Transactions of the Dumfriesshire and Galloway Natural History and Antiquarian Society* (1862–).
*Thirds of Benefices:* *Accounts of the Collectors of Thirds of Benefices 1561–1572*, ed. G. Donaldson (SHS, 1949).
Thompson, *Carthusian Order:* E. M. Thompson, *The Carthusian Order in England* (London, 1930).
Todd, 'Dunblane Diocese': J. R. Todd, 'Pre-Reformation Cure of Souls in Dunblane Diocese', *IR*, 26 (1975), pp. 27–42.
TSES: *Transactions of the Scottish Ecclesiological Society* (1903–).
Verschuur, 'Perth Charterhouse': M. B. Verschuur, 'The Perth Charterhouse in the Sixteenth Century', *IR*, 39 (1988), pp. 1–11.
*Vet. Mon.:* *Vetera Monumenta Hibernorum et Scotorum Historiam Illustrantia*, ed. A. Theiner (Rome, 1864).
Watt, *Fasti:* D. E. R. Watt, *Fasti Ecclesiae Scoticanae Medii Aevi* (SRS, 1969).
Webster, *Dunfermline:* J. M. Webster, *Dunfermline Abbey* (Dunfermline, 1948).
*Wigt. Chrs:* *Wigtownshire Charters*, ed. R. C. Reid (SHS, 1960).
Winning, 'Church Councils': T. Winning, 'Church Councils in Sixteenth-Century Scotland', in McRoberts, *Essays*, pp. 332–58.

# Index

*A surname without a forename denotes the family; with a forename it denotes an individual.*